Anna Perdriau

Speaking

to Hearts and Minds

This is an IndieMosh book
brought to you by MoshPit Publishing
an imprint of Mosher's Business Support Pty Ltd
PO BOX 147
Hazelbrook NSW 2779
www.indiemosh.com.au

Cataloguing-in-Publication entry is available from the National Library of Australia: http://catalogue.nla.gov.au/

Title: Speaking to Hearts and Minds - Public Speaking to engage, energise and elevate for Government and Corporate Executives
Author: Perdriau, Anna
ISBNS: 978-1-925447-57-6 (paperback)
             978-1-925447-58-3 (ebook – epub)
             978-1-925447-59-0 (ebook – mobi)

Cover design by Anna Perdriau, author, and Ally Mosher, IndieMosh.

Anna Perdriau

Speaking
to Hearts and Minds

Testimonials

'Anna is a sponge! She is an amazing student of the art of public speaking. On stage Anna has a delightfully positive presence. Listen to what she has to say!'

Darren LaCroix
2001 World Champion of Public Speaking
darrenlacroix.com

'Anna Perdriau is like her writing: helpful, entertaining, fun and full of speaking expertise based on deep experience and high-level training. Anna and her book are recommended wholeheartedly.'

Rodney Marks
comedian.com.au

'Anna is a very engaging and highly knowledgeable speaking coach, trainer, and mentor. She is clearly dedicated, enthusiastic, and professional: and coupled with her sharp analytical mind knows how to get results. Highly recommended.'

Eric Pace
highperformancethinking.com

'This is a must-read if you're ready to step-up and wield real influence in your life as Anna reveals the secrets that will truly connect you with the hearts and minds of your audience.'

Phil Preston
philpreston.co

'I've had the pleasure of working with Anna on the chapter leadership team of Professional Speakers Australia. I have found Anna to be skilled and professional in both her 'front of house' and 'behind the scenes' work. She is consistent, reliable and committed. You can trust her to deliver!'

Karen Armstrong
https://www.karenarmstrong.com.au

'As a Project Director Anna held significant responsibility in shaping the delivery of a complex Government program. Anna demonstrated exceptional communication skills and a particular ability to analyse the details and concisely present complex information to high level decision bodies in a clear, concise and relevant manner. I recommend Anna as an outstanding communicator and leader with integrity.'

Ivan Zlabur
Senior Executive Service, Australian Government

Contents

Coaching: the fastest way to excellence

Introduction

When is your next speech?

Regardless of whether it is tomorrow or three months' time, there lies a golden opportunity to lift your audience.

This book is written for you if you strive for better connections with your audience. It is for people who know that there is value to add to an audience, and that every word and action has an impact on your audience.

Delivering a presentation is like going on a first date. Your audience wants to feel a connection, and making one wrong move or word could prove fatal. It doesn't take much for a gesture to be misinterpreted. (Note: if you haven't been on a first date in many years, because you have been married, this still applies. I recommend you invite your spouse on a date - to get yourself in practice. Analyse your experience and how it can apply to speaking to an audience for the first time. Alternatively, keep reading.)

'Speaking to hearts and minds' is a phrase that means speaking is an art that can constantly be refined and improved. Speaking is not a matter of do once and have it mastered. It is more of a journey. A journey that goes hand in hand with your own personal development journey. As a leader, a project manager, a speaker, an influencer, a human.

This book is both educational and experiential. That means, you can read to learn, and you can interact with the material to consider how it applies to your speaking situation.

I draw your attention to a speaking spectrum below. At one end is 'Avoid' in the middle is 'Comfortable' and at the other end is 'Excel'. I invite you to consider, where do you sit?

[_____]

Avoid   Comfortable   Excellence

One of the following statements may apply to you:

- I've been speaking to audiences for years. I'm comfortable in doing so.

- I hate public speaking and avoid it at all costs.

- I don't need to speak up, no-one will listen anyway.

Do any of these sound familiar to you? If not, jot down your reaction to the topic.

While serving in the Australian Government, I felt privileged to be among the company of some of the most brilliant minds in Australia. Experts in military strategy, weapons technology, nuclear physicists, even rocket scientists. I sat through many a technical presentation. Some of them went above my head, despite dedicated efforts to focus. Even if you were an expert in that field you may end up confused. This was because the speaker had not considered there to be one point, one key message their audience could walk away with and be all the better for. Or if there were multiple messages, they were not presented in a way of crystal clear clarity.

When I started in the early 1990s, those around me were male, middle aged and wearing a grey suit (a stereotype I know, some wore black suits). It was in the days before diversity. As an ambitious female aged in her 20s, I was definitely different. I stuck out like a sore thumb. Despite this interesting dynamic, I pushed through. I felt compelled to do so. As I learnt more, it became clearer to me that I could add a lot of value. Through being different and offering a difference, I started to make progress. I found a way to contribute and a manner in which to do so. In those days admittedly I could not be radically different. That would not have worked. A bit different with a lot of same seemed to be ok. I had to tap into my instincts to get a sense of how I was being received and that I was 'blending in' the right amount. (Isn't it funny that you should have a certain amount of 'sameness' so that you can be different?).

One day it hit me. What I possessed was the ability to communicate with clarity. I worked harder than anyone I knew. I'm not trying to blow my own trumpet. It was that I thought differently. Above all, I listened. I spent time listening to people who perhaps were not the most succinct conversationalists, because they had so much brilliant technical knowledge to share, but who really knew what they were talking about. I wanted to understand the exact point, the kernel of what they were saying. I wouldn't stop until I understood. If it meant drilling in and asking more questions, that's what I did. I put in the time to understand them to find the gold nugget of wisdom they were offering. Through understanding, I gained my edge.

Over time, my urge to use this edge intensified. I didn't even realise it at the time but I would often be critiquing the effectiveness of the leaders in my organisation on their ability to succinctly summarise their point, to communicate effectively and with impact, and whether they did so with variety and flair. If they did, I would always make a point of commending them or complimenting their abilities. Sadly though, these moments were not common. One example of this was when I heard Mike Pezzulo speak. At the time he was a rising leader in the Australian Government. I made sure I sent him an email giving him positive feedback and he replied positively too, albeit frank. His career eventually soared. (I don't conclude it was due to my email.)

There were many people who did not have the ability to be succinct. It doesn't have to continue this way though. Being a servant of the Australian people does not limit you to only wearing a grey suit, being male and a certain age and having 2.4 kids. (For the international or younger audience members or those with fuzzy memories, there used to be a television advertisement in Australia which pointed out that the average Australian household had 2.4 kids, which seemed to stick!). Those days of much sameness are gone. Not that there is anything to fault about such statistics, it's more that nowadays we are wiser about the value of difference in all its various shapes and forms.

Regardless of your age group, ethnicity or gender, my hope for you is that you will embrace speaking. The more that I learn about speaking the more I find out there is to discover. Because much like setting a personal challenge, such as climbing a mountain, running a marathon or doing a charity ball, you learn much about yourself through the journey.

What is interesting about the speaking journey, is that as much as when you start speaking in front of an audience, it is very much about you. When you lose the issues that plague you in the beginning however, like the nerves and the worry and mindset issues, your focus starts to shift from you to your audience member. Each and every one of them. If you take this too far however, you can become disappointed in the event not every audience member likes your presentation. What's key is did you impact those you needed to.

The dynamic here is that to speak to your audience is to serve them. When making it about your audience, there is less need for you to hold on to worry for yourself.

Within the past five years there were some surveys undertaken in 26 countries around the world, where the presentation skills of leaders in organisations were examined. The results showed that the top three highest complaints from the audience were consistently listed as:

1. **Too much information** - as Craig Valentine would say 'squeeze too much information in, you squeeze your audience out'.

2. **Not relevant** - it was probably very relevant to the Speaker, but they had not put it into the right frame of reference for the audience so they didn't think it was for them.

3. **No point** - it wasn't targeted and they saw it as a waste of their time.

To me, it is very easy to believe these remarks. As they are consistent with what I have experienced working in large organisations for more than 20 years. These were precisely the types of feedback comment I would hear. Typical comments were 'that was a total waste of 40 minutes' or even worse 'there's two hours of my life I'll never get back'. Not sure about you, but I don't want to live my life regretting what I am doing.

And let's face it, some people _are_ difficult to engage. They are naturally going to resist the idea of change, because it is easier to do so. It is much easier for them to cruise along. Fortunately, those days are well and truly behind us.

Whether it's small business or big. *Every*one must pull their weight.

The good news. We can change this situation. You can reach those people and engage them. What I have also learnt is that most people want to do a good job. They usually just need some clarity around that. That can be all it will take to raise them up and allow them to shine and make a difference to you.

EVERY speech is a golden opportunity for you to further mould and shape your people and your results.

The wonderful thing here is that <u>*you*</u> are committed to making that happen. You see that this is your role as a leader and you are stepping up to make it so.

Unlimited Speaking

My aim is for you to have an unlimited speaking ability. To know how and when you can speak with an audience. Rather than hindered or afraid. In other words be prepared for your next presentation. Be comfortable and confident to step up and speak to any audience and to have the tools in your kit to draw upon. Most importantly, to be able to dazzle, thrill and educate your audience shifting them and lifting them to new heights.

The word '*Unlimited*' is about lifting you up, removing boundaries and having you soar the skies. It's erasing all of the perceived or real threats to what has previously stopped you from delivering an engaging and enthralling presentation. The only limits that exist for your speaking are in fact the ones that you place on yourself. So [insert sound of magic wand] let's free you up to be all you can be and let you loose on your people. Then when the opportunities present, or when you seek them out, you can shine.

This book is dedicated to leaders who speak. Specifically, leaders who serve in Government and Corporate environments; executives and crusaders who want to progress their presentation skills so that you can be received as the leader that you are.

This is what I want to bring in this book. How people in organisations can cut to their key core and communicate effectively in their speaking endeavours.

This book is for those who:

- have been speaking in front of people for many years, but who also want to revitalise their skills so that they can go from the 'old way' of speaking to the 'new way'

- are afraid of or not comfortable to speak

- want to inject fun and interaction into their presentations.

The old way is the way it used to always be done. You know the person talking at the front of the room. They impart their knowledge, so much knowledge that it is too much. They do this in such a manner that it is so hard to keep track of what is what. There might be really interesting information being presented but it is moving too quickly to really sink in. They use a lot of data, information (overload) and statistics not put into context. There is impressive knowledge but sadly it is not presented in a way the audience can respond, engage and feel excited about it. In fact, it is well, boring. Let's wave goodbye to the old way. *Bye Bye old way!*

The new way: Have you ever seen a speaker who is exciting? This is where the speaker engages first. They might ask you to answer a question, discuss a topic with your neighbour or enthrall you in a story that has message and meaning. The new way involves interaction in a way that leaves the audience feeling engaged, inspired and energised to go and change themselves.

Why should I be excited about new developments in public speaking?

Here's the thing. Most people hate even the thought of public speaking, because they feel awkward. They don't like having the audience look at them because they might make a mistake, forget what they wanted to say, get flustered, turn bright red, get tongue tied, and the list goes on.

So what if public speaking is no longer about being 'looked at' by your audience. Or an activity that doesn't need you to be riddled with fear. When you make your presentation an engaging experience you change the whole dynamic.

Let's look into this a little further. Here are some words that people associate with how they feel about public speaking, or the idea of doing public speaking, now:

- Petrifying

- Terrifying

- Scary

- Nerve-wracking

- Heart pounding

- Embarrassing

- Awkward

Pretty ugly set of words. If you were an alien who arrived on planet earth and asked what public speaking is and were confronted with that set of words, you probably would not want to be going there in a hurry.

On the other hand, here is another set of words that can also be associated with public speaking:

- FUN   *(yes and doesn't this word deserve to be in capital letters?)*

- Engaging

- Entertaining

- Interactive

- Serve others

- Gratifying

- Purposeful

- Educating

- Enriching

- Creative

- Innovative

- Exploratory

- Fantastic

- Bettering humankind

(notice the list for the good stuff is actually longer?...)

Isn't that exciting? No longer does the attention have to be on you. Do you know what this means?.... it means you are freed up - to be the fabulous *You* that your friends know you as. It means you no longer should feel the need to hold back. It means that you can view speaking in a new light, in a refreshing manner, without the boundaries that may have previously been holding you back before.

This is so cool it's not even funny. By shifting the emphasis off you and onto your audience, you can enjoy the process of public speaking through expert facilitation. All you need to know now is simply how to engage your audience.....the rest is up to them.

This is the new way. It is a new wave sweeping speaking and it is here to stay.

I am living proof that with effective communication and speaking skills, you can embrace your speaking, find that you can go from Voice to Victory and achieve unlimited speaking success.

From Voice to Victory:
Anna's 3 Vs Methodology

The methodology I use as a platform to branch out for all of my teachings is the 'Three Vs' to take yourself from Voice to Victory. Here is a breakdown of the three Vs:

V1: When you make your speech All About Audience you add Value to your audience.

V2: When you bring out the 'real you' in your speech in an authentic way, you bring them Veritas.

V3: Being the sound that carries the message, key to your success in speaking is your Voice.

VALUE – gift you bring

The first V is Value. This is all about the gift you bring to your audience. Specifically:

<u>To GIFT is to LIFT.</u>

Let's go into it further.

We speak for a reason. We don't only speak for the fun of it. We speak for a purpose. To gift as a speaker is to skilfully craft what you know so that it is of value to your audience.

Imagine two cliff tops with a body of water in between. At the moment we cannot cross that on foot. Imagine that on one side you have what you know. Your knowledge. On the other side you have your audience, your people, your tribe. The people you want to serve with your message and knowledge.

Now imagine that your speech is going to be like a bridge that links the two. Your speaking is going to bring them to new awareness or understanding or knowledge levels. You are giving them a lot. The ability to take them from where they are now, to that new place. Because you are the Agent of Change. Serving their needs.

It is taking what you know, your knowledge and building a bridge between it and what they need. It is bridging the gap. To your audience's needs.

I invite you to ask yourself. What's the Gift I will bring to my audience?

Is it:

- <u>A key learning</u> - something new they need to know or learn, or further clarity on something they know about, but could do with more understanding of. For example it may be a rather complex issue, that if simplified, if broken down to its components and explained, they could understand better.

- <u>To elevate them</u> - people want to be part of a community that elevates them. People want to feel valued. With your speaking you may wish to bring your people closer together and even create a stronger bonded community. Challenge them to innovate for example.

- <u>New information</u> - your take on a concept or subject. By letting them in on your thoughts on a topic, they understand you and your values better.

* *What's the Gift you will bring?* Take some time to really think about it.

The first V was about the Value you bring.

VERITAS - who you are

Bring more 'You' into your speaking.

When you bring You, and when you understand You, you by default, give confidence to others to find themselves.

By being yourself, you can help them to step outside and find themselves.

Show them who you are and what you represent, not just what you know, being in the position you are in. Show them who you are, not just what you do.

In 2005 when I was working in the government as a project director, as a development requirement I participated in a leadership program. We had to perform a number of tasks, for example, a presentation, a report, prioritising a set of tasks etc, and then we received feedback.

When it came to the presentation, I gave mine and then at the end I was goofing around and laughing with the panel of experts who had analysed me. At one point I said something and burst out laughing, at which point they said 'that's what we would like you to do more of in the presentation'. I had wanted to gain credibility so much that I had been far too serious in my presenting and they wanted to see more of my personality.

An interesting lesson.

Here are two key ways on how to workshop bringing more You:

*You - * what are 3 words that describe your personality and branding?*

_____

_____

_____

*Story - * what story or stories (with a lesson) will you use to support your Gift?*

_____

_____

_____

_____

Answering these questions and writing down your answers will help to get to know yourself better in terms of what you can bring to your speaking.

The other elements of Veritas I'd like to mention here (which are fleshed out more in the chapters within this book) are:

- <u>Connecting with your audience using body</u> - your body and how you move, stand, breathe and gesture right down to your eyes, smile, laughter (where possible and where appropriate) and pause. (Refer Chapter 7 - entice vocally)

- <u>Managing your mindset</u> - this starts with how you think about yourself. We need to have you in a balanced and positive frame of mind. That you are there to serve above all else. You must know and believe that you deserve to be there and that you have an important mission. We have all had negative comments put to us throughout our life - whether a parent, teacher or someone along the line who told you that you couldn't, that you aren't good enough, smart enough, pretty, funny (insert word: 'not __ enough') etc. You need to address any of those issues and know within yourself that you are good enough to be there and that you have a critical mission to perform. (Refer Chapter 2 - expand mindset)

- <u>Your mind's eye</u> - this is all about what your mind is focused on and your internal dialogue. You want your mind to not go into fight or flight mode. Your mind will go searching for answers. Questions your mind may be asking could be 'Will I remember what I need to say?' needs to be framed differently to be 'How will I deliver the best possible speech to my audience?' (Refer Chapter 2 - expand mindset)

This is the essence of the second V, VERITAS.

VOICE - how you deliver

Your voice is yours and truly unique. Like your fingerprints. It helps to bring You (Veritas) to life.

What you want to do with your voice is to nurture it so that you can:

- Bring it out

- Make it vibrant

- Use it to compel and to incite emotion, passion and power in your speaking

The way you use your Voice should be based upon your aspects of Value and Veritas. Your voice brings life and credibility to the other 2 Vs.

This is all about using your voice intentionally. Your message can be delivered with absolute clarity using and honing your voice.

The types of considerations for the checklist of reviewing yourself includes such points as follows:

- <u>volume</u> - how soft to how loud you speak. You can speak softly to bring gentleness to a delicate story.

- <u>pitch</u> - how low to how high you speak. The higher you speak the more you can bring out emotions in your voice.

- <u>rate</u> - how slow to how fast you speak. I inject a lot of pauses into my speech and speak slower. Remember pauses are a vocabulary. They do a lot.

Your voice is critical to bringing out the life in your speaking - to match your leadership style and your message.

Also, your breathing in how you speak is key to effectiveness.

Diagram 1 – The 3 Vs to gain Victory Via Voice:

Everything you will read in this book, is an expansion of the three Vs. Represented here as a model:

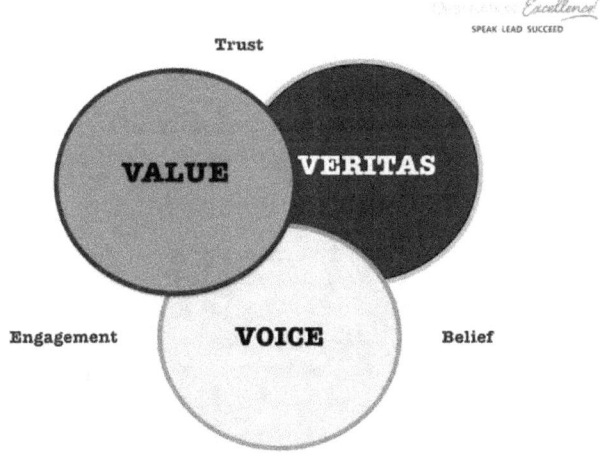

This book is for you to experience how you want. You don't have to read it from left to right. You can experiment with various topics and complete the exercises in each chapter. At the back of the book is my public speaking alphabet, containing principles you can apply.

What's important is that this book is a guide to help you along, to build your ability, to stretch you to the new place that you know you are truly capable to arrive at.

Speakers: spread your wings and soar the skies. I'll be with you along the way.

www.speakingexcellence.co

anna@destinationexcellence.com.au

Chapter 1:

Engage

'Let's ban boring,
forge through fear,
and have FUN.'

Anna Perdriau

Chapter 1: Engage

Make your presentation All About Audience

Friday 17th August.

The Golden Gavel dinner at International Convention for Public Speaking in Orlando, Florida. I was sitting at my table eagerly awaiting the after dinner speaker.

I could hear the chatter of 2200 people and could feel their excitement over the big name speaker who was about to address us. As I devoured the last bite of my tiramisu, the MC introduced the much-anticipated speaker.

The speaker that night was fascinating. Sitting calmly on his stool, with a glass of water and small palm cards, he spoke to me. Like we were having a one to one conversation.

The speaker that night changed me.

The speaker that night gave me a gift. The gift of finding my life purpose.

That speaker was John Maxwell.

John Maxwell did this by bringing something to that audience that we could benefit from. Something of value.

Yes it's true, some people in that audience had heard the message before. Maybe they hadn't acted on it, or needed that reminder. Or if they had already found the purpose of their life, it could serve as a solid checkpoint.

That night John Maxwell offered me a gift. I've been pursuing my dream ever since.

Here's the thing. What John Maxwell did for me, I can do for you. And you can do for others.

Over to you. If you do nothing else when speaking to an audience in the future, you need to do this one thing.

You need to put the needs of your audience first. By doing so, you'll add value to each person in that audience.

Do this by giving them a gift when you speak.

How do you give this gift of adding value to your audience?

What not to do

The first thing to do is avoid the trap that many new (and experienced) speakers fall into, which is to think about what they want to say, or take what they know, and then start writing a speech around that. Many speakers NEVER test whether what they are bringing to their audience is of relevance to them.

The first imperative is to understand your audience.

It's that simple. Get to know your audience. Know them so that you recognise what is important to them. Understand what drives them.

Ten ways to get to know your audience

Here are ten ways to help you understand your audience so that you can tailor your message especially for them:

Ask

If you can have access to them beforehand, or at least the person engaging you to speak to them, make sure you ask 'What is your greatest pain point?'

In 2014 I attended a networking event for female entrepreneurs. There was a buzz in the air (*Note: When women entrepreneurs gather and they have had time to prepare, preen and put on their pumps, there is no stopping the energy.*).

We were about to head into the main room for the presentation when a lady came up to introduce herself. It turned out to be the main speaker, Mary. Mary asked each of the three of us in this conversation a question. 'What is your greatest pain point right now?' She then intently listened to our answers and acknowledged via feedback.

I was impressed. As a speaker Mary went out of her way to seek input from each person in the room. Now I'm fairly certain that Mary was already prepared with her content (and her subject matter knowledge) sufficiently that she was already addressing the issues that we entrepreneurs were facing. But the fact that she used the process of doing this 'mini-interview' technique, showed me she was on the front foot.

Mary was on the ball. Mary cared what her audience had at the front of their mind.

What questions can you ask to understand your audience?

_____

_____

_____

_____

_____

Buy them a coffee – use this opportunity to ask questions.

We live in a cafe society. People enjoy doing business over a coffee. It is not the stuffy formal boardroom style. I guess it is the closest to them feeling like they are not 'at work'.

If possible, an informal chat over coffee is a great way to better understand your audience. Though not always possible to chat directly to the source, the actual audience members, that's the ideal target.

If you cannot talk to them directly, talk to the event planner. If you're presenting to your staff, and want to understand what issues they are facing, you could try contacting the people they report to, which may be the people who report to you. For example, you may have directors reporting to you and those directors have teams of staff reporting to them.

By all means meet for coffee with each director one on one. Note also though, that this person doesn't necessarily always know the hot buttons within their team (though, arguably, they should). This person could indeed be the problem. If this is the case, they won't necessarily share the same perspective as their team members.

In this example, I would meet for coffee both with some team members as well as the director.

How can I apply this?

_____

_____

_____

_____

Research their industry.

Find out what is topical in their field of expertise.

In this scenario you have been asked to present at an industry conference. The conference will have a theme. Investigate.

Then investigate further. Don't stay in your own patch. Find out what is happening more broadly and then consider what you might speak about and how this impacts on the industry trend. Build your presentation concept and content so that it's clear, relevant and insightful. Remember, as a speaker you are an agent of change. Your audience will relax in the knowledge that you know what you are talking about.

Hypothetical: I work in the Australian Taxation Office (ATO) as a senior executive and have been asked to present at a Leadership convention for whole of government. Various government departments will be there. Although my topic is leadership in the ATO, I will, of course, be researching what is going on beyond my own department in this space. The results could then be represented in my presentation by having a slide with a comparison of the various departments and how they are progressing in this area. Hence, the presentation of my information has broader applicability because it is not simply ATO centric. This is like the difference between presenting data to left brain, other than right brain, thinkers. You want to have variety in your presented data. You want to show that you are up-to-date with the industry as well as your subject matter. Your audience will expect you to have the same approach as every other speaker. Surprise them.

How can I apply this?

_____

_____

_____

_____

_____

Find out statistics about them.

What makes them unique? Acknowledge this in your speech.

Your audience loves nothing more but to learn something about themselves. Let them in on the learning.

For example, if they are accountants, find out the latest research about accountants. Love their numbers as much as they do. Then, discover from your perspective how that is fascinating. Include this in your presentation. This can also be an opportunity for light hearted humour. Example: you discover some research showing that accountants are the most caring of the technical professions. You could show a slide with this data presented, make a comment along the lines, 'so if you are not an accountant, just be warned that come morning tea break, the following could happen' followed by the next slide with a funny image of a large group of people hugging. Then you can say 'I'm just warning you out, ok?' Of course, delivering such a piece requires some personality and persona to bring it to life. Put some animation into it and practice it in front of people and get feedback before you do. Or run it by your presentation skills coach.

There are opportunities for you to engage your audience by tapping in to what makes them unique. All this takes is some research + preparation + practice + feedback + improvement. You can bring your audience closer to you as a result. They'll love it.

How can I apply this?

_____

_____

_____

_____

_____

_____

Research their competitors and uncover both the similarities and differences between them.

This is a very useful technique enabling you to demonstrate your courage as a leader and presenter.

Competitor research can be a delicate subject when you have competing firms in your audience. They don't want to be exposed for any weakness they may have, nor would you want to embarrass. You want to respect them. After all, you are the expert and they want to learn and be inspired by you. Which is why you can take another approach to this. Instead you could allude to companies in other industries. This can relieve tension that may otherwise exist between competitors.

Case in point: you work in the roads and maritime industry. The leadership issue you want to talk about relates to safety. So rather than use safety examples solely from this industry, such as traffic statistics, which you could do and are probably already well known, you might compare them to examples in other industries. For example, military accidents, spills from the oil and gas industry or the window cleaning business. You can use these examples to weave a thread.

What is most important here is that the comparison must be relevant and lead to the fundamental point you want to make. Which could be as simple as 'Paying Attention Pays'.

There it is. Your 'Foundational Phrase'. (<u>Note</u>: read all about your Foundational Phrase in chapter 8.)

How can I apply this?

_____

_____

_____

_____

_____

_____

Find out what they value, what they care about and what matters to them.

How on earth could you possibly know what one person in your audience is thinking, let alone hundreds or thousands?

Easy. When you put it into perspective, when you break it down, we are all human beings first. We give our attention to whatever we feel like caring about as humans. Like doing the things that we enjoy such as holidays and spending time with family. As opposed to spending all of our time at work.

Then, if we work in a particular field or industry, we are likely to care about certain aspects of this, like progressing it to make things easier. Using technology to save time and money. For example, people in the speaking industry used to have to painstakingly write out their speeches longhand before the advent of typewriters, word processors and computers allowed them to be typed easily, whereas now there are tools where you can dictate the words and they are automatically produced on screen. There are also tools that take your words and create you a PowerPoint slide pack of images!

What is that thing for your audience that they care about progressing? Is it taking the next step to automate the systems in your organisation? Let's just say you are at a crossroads with a new system to be introduced. You can discuss here the fundamental principles that matter in making such a decision, rather than the solution itself, which has the potential to cause tension and detract from your message.

Something else they may value is resourcing. A common issue today is when we have to ask our people to continuously improve and 'do more with less'. If this is truly the case for what you need from them and you know what they care about is their health and wellbeing, you must make your speech so that it addresses that thing they are most worried about. I remember a presentation from a leader to his team of approximately 100 people. Resourcing was an issue. I was disappointed when the leader merely concurred with the opinion of the audience in that there was nothing he or they could do to help the resourcing situation. STOP doing this leaders! This is not leadership! This is not inspiring hope for a better world. This is taking the easy way out, demotivating your team, settling for mediocrity and you don't want to do that. Your audience could walk out of that presentation feeling flat.

This requires thought and planning on your part. Consider what your people fear, how can you put them at ease by offering different ways to address and improve a given situation, and afterwards, inspire them with hope!

Find out what it is that your audience values and give it to them.

How can I apply this?

_____

_____

_____

_____

_____

_____

Research topics they are into and what matters to them, e.g. science developments.

Ok, so you don't know about a topic to the degree that your audience does. Research it! Go to a level of effort to know more. Don't say you haven't the time. You do. If you really don't, you shouldn't be speaking to this audience. Delegate something to your team and get to what's important. You must hit the mark when speaking with your people.

In this example you are presenting to a group of people not like you. Shorten the gap, in fact close it. Take your perspective, learn about this topic and deliver them content in a fresh way. Imagine you are a baby boomer presenting to a group of millennials. The old way of presenting would be to do the blah blah blah at them. The new way could be to demonstrate how 1960s music is like scientific developments.

Make it fresh, interesting and still you.

A note about delegation: A large part of successful delegation is giving your people the belief that they can do something. This drives their motivation. If they sense that you don't trust them to carry out a responsibility, they won't respect it. If they believe however, that you have the confidence in them to achieve an outcome such as deliver a task or a project, having given them the responsibility and trusting them, they are more likely to rise to it. The same goes in presenting. If you talk at the audience, rather than demonstrate you believe in them, you won't have the same impact.

How can I apply this?

_____

_____

_____

_____

_____

_____

Ask questions during your speech, 'hand up if you...'

Asking questions of your audience is sometimes done incorrectly. The only reason you should be polling your audience is.......(drumroll)....... because you care about what they are going to say! There's nothing worse than a speaker who poses a question, has the audience raise their hand, and then promptly ignores it. No no no.

Having got that out of the way, this is a great technique for developing audience engagement. The correct way to question is to do so when you want to determine how many people in your audience think about, feel or do something in relation to the question. Such as asking 'hand up if you are working more than 50/60/70 hours each week?' This is a yes / no question which they can easily consider and answer. Your hypothetical question must always have a purpose.

The wording of the question is important. I learnt from Craig Valentine (World Champion of Public Speaking) that you should never ask 'how many of you...' because that is a clumsy reference to a theoretical group which creates a barrier between you and your audience. It's an 'us and them' approach to posing questions. Make it a direct 'you' focused question, 'hands up if you, raise your hand if you...' etc. According to Neuro Linguistic Programming (NLP) the word 'You' is entirely important because people love to hear that you are talking to them.

The next step is what you do with the responses. If 90% of the audience raise their hand in reply, acknowledge that. Feed it back to them. Don't just look and say 'uh-huh'. Inform the audience 'Ok, that's approximately 90% in the room who are working more than 50 hours per week. What this tells me is... and what I think we should do about this is...'.

Make the point as to why you have asked. Then use the information appropriately and to support your approach to your speech.

This approach works well when you have some flexibility to adapt your presentation and the activities involved on the day. It does not work well if you have based your presentation on the notion that people are not overworked and your poll demonstrates that they are in fact working a lot longer hours than you had assumed.

Asking questions can be powerful when you know the outcome you want to achieve and can conduct the session based on any answer whether anticipated or not.

How can I apply this?

_____

_____

_____

_____

_____

_____

Ask them to rate where they are in three categories, i.e. beginner, intermediate, advanced.

This can be a fun, light-hearted interaction with your audience serving as a way to engage them and energise the room. It's a great technique I've seen done by Dr Rich Allen. It is also a means to find out where your audience 'sees' themselves in their own mind and in terms of their expertise. This is achieved via a quick poll.

How it works. You pick three things, probably associated with basic, intermediate and advanced levels of your topic. Then pick three labels that are much more interesting labels that people would want to relate to. For example, you might choose animals: mouse - monkey - elephant. You might choose cars: mini - commodore - van. Or: sparrow - galah - eagle. It is not about which one they like, it is to do with their expertise, so explain it first. Then instruct your audience as follows: 'Let's get some idea of where you think you are in your level of expertise. I ask you to first consider which group you are in, from the basic level to the intermediate level or the advanced level, represented by these three animal categories - if you are a mouse (basic level, new to this up to one year) stand on the left side of the room. If you are a monkey you have intermediate level knowledge (between 1-5 years) and should stand at the back. Or if you are an elephant in terms of your knowledge on this subject (10+ years) stand to the right hand side of the room.'

Again while this activity is engaging, quick and fun, it is imperative that you frame it in the right way so as to get the best response from the participants. This activity works best for a workshop style presentation where there is space enough for them to move around, though it certainly can work in practically any venue set-up. (Note: you could also then add up the amount of years of expertise in the room - the audience will be impressed with themselves.)

How can I apply this?

_____

_____

_____

_____

_____

Brainstorm activity.

Uncover the 'group think' of the audience. Identify what the collective thinking within this audience is. Then consider what you have that can help them address this.

This is best approached with skill in interaction. It will also involve some quick thinking and adaptation depending on what the results are. You will in effect be conducting a facilitation role and steering things in a particular direction.

I hear you ask 'But Anna, what if they are a broad audience of people from all different places?'

Yes I understand you may have a diverse audience. They will still have, however, a common thread between them. So your research for them will simply be a matter of finding the 'macro' level elements that tie them together. If you are having trouble, try starting at the top and working down.

Break it down:

Human beings

Live in Australia + Sydney

Business people

Interested in being successful in business

When it comes to brainstorming, this is really a creative process of gathering ideas and recording them, on say, a whiteboard. One technique I learned from John Pastorelli is to go further than you normally would do. What this means is rather than going for say, 10 ideas, set a quota of 30 ideas to be collected. You keep collecting them until you get this many. This will tease out unique ideas which would have normally not surfaced, but could be just the ones you go with.

It can be hard to do. You just have to not settle for less than the 30 ideas and keep going until you collect that many, or more. The gold is hiding in the unexpected, so keep going!

The reason for this is because you never know what will come out in the process. New ideas, fresh takes. It all helps.

By collecting the 30 ideas on the whiteboard you can then ask the audience to put into categories and then tease out what it is they want to talk about. Then take it from there.

What is important here is that when you conduct this activity, keep it moving and keep it dynamic, so as to maintain your audience's attention.

Then ultimately show the point for you working through this. It's a bit like problem solving and analysis in an interactive and unfolding way.

An example of what you could uncover here:

Audience Attributes	Identifying Gap	Gap	VALUE
Human beings Live in Australia Sydney Business people Interested in being successful in business	What they need to know + Your unique knowledge	How to succeed in business Cost cutting techniques	How to cut your costs by 30%

Voila! You know how to become successful in business specifically (or through a specific method) and therefore, by showing them how to do this, you can bring Value that is relevant to this audience.

How can I apply this?

_____

_____

_____

_____

_____

_____

These engagement techniques will enable you to connect. When you make your presentation 'All About Audience', you give your audience Value.

These 10 techniques range from methods that you can use prior to your presentation and to help you prepare, through practices applied during your presentation, to skilled facilitation with your audience.

Here is a summary table for the 10 ways to get to know your audience.

Table 1 – top 10 ways to get to know your audience

1	Ask to have pre-event access	Ask If you can have access to them beforehand, or at least the person engaging you to speak to them, make sure you ask what their greatest pain point is. You can also do this directly before the event in the networking. This way you make sure you are tuned in to them and can shift your approach accordingly.

2	Chat over a Coffee	Coffee n' Chat
		We live in a cafe society. Use this opportunity to ask questions to find out what they need. People enjoy doing business over a coffee. It is not the stuffy formal boardroom style. I guess it is the closest to them feeling like they are not at 'work'.
		If possible, chat over a coffee is a great way to better understand your audience. Not always possible to chat direct to the source, the actual audience members, but it is ideal.
3	Research their Industry	Research their industry.
		Find out what is topical in their field of expertise.
		In this scenario you have been asked to present at an industry conference. The conference will have a theme. Investigate.
		Then investigate further. Don't stay in your own patch. Find out what is happening more broadly and then consider how what you do ties in and impacts on the trend.
4	Find out their stats	Find out statistics about them:
		What makes them unique? Acknowledge this in your speech.
		Your audience loves nothing more but to learn something about themselves. Let them in on the learning.

5	Research their competitors	Research their competitors: To uncover what is the same and what is different. This is a useful technique to enable you to demonstrate your courage as a leader and presenter. This can be a delicate subject when you have competing firms in your audience. They don't want to be exposed for any weakness they may have, nor would you want to embarrass your audience. You want to treat them respectfully. Use this one as a generic reference point.
6	Find out what they value	Find out what they value: How on earth could you possibly know what one person in your audience is thinking, let alone hundreds or thousands? Easy. When you put it into perspective, when you break it down, we are all human beings first. We care about what we feel like caring about as humans. Remember this.
7	Research Topics	Research topics they are into and what matters to them: When you don't know about a topic that your audience does. Research it. Go to a level of effort to know more. Don't say you don't have time. You do. If you really don't, you shouldn't be speaking to your audience. Delegate something to your team and get to what's important. You must hit the mark when

		speaking with your people. Bring your audience closer to your topic through connecting it to theirs.
8	Asking questions	Ask you audience a question like 'hand up if you like chocolate?'
		The correct way to question is to do so when you want to gauge how many people in your audience think about, feel or do something in relation to the question. Such as asking 'hand up if you are working more than 40 hours each week?'. This is a yes / no question which they can easily consider and answer.
9	Ask them to rate	An interactive fun activity.
		Pick three items that represent levels associated with basic, intermediate and advanced levels of your topic. Then pick three labels that are much more interesting labels that people would want to relate to. For example, you might choose animals: mouse - monkey - elephant. You might choose cars: mini - commodore - van.
10	Brainstorm activity	Uncover the 'group think' of the audience. Identify what the collective thinking from this audience is. Then consider what you have that can help them to address.

In addition to these engagement techniques, it is of course mandatory to connect with your audience via your content. Here are some top ways to leave an impact.

Table 2 – Top 5 ways to leave an impact

Make 'em laugh	Engage with humour	If you don't already have humour in your stories and / or your material, you can add some. You may want to add more humour even when you already have some. Easier said than done, but humour specialists can help. Remember though, you know funny stuff that has happened in your life and you can bring this into your presentations. You don't have to be a comedian, you can entertain with humour that has filled your everyday life.
Make 'em cry	Pull on their heartstrings	We have all been drawn in to a heart-wrenching story that tugged at our emotions. I know I have, and there wasn't a dry eye in the house. Not everyone believes they have a story that can achieve this with an audience, but I believe an effective speaker can tell a heartstrings story and have this impact.

Make 'em feel better	About themselves	We all want to feel good. This is pretty much the quest of life. The reason why people finish their day at work and then sit in front of the telly to chillax. Because it feels good. They don't have to try, nor stress, they just forget their worries for that little short burst. The same reason as knowing that you shouldn't eat that chocolate bar but doing it all the same because it feels nice and it feels good to do so. When you tell feel-good stories or tales that touch them, this is a key driver in engaging them.
Make 'em learn	Something new	One of the things that excites people and gets them buying things is when they learn something about themselves that they didn't already know. An insight, a reason, a habit, a pattern. If it makes your audience have an 'ah-ha' lightbulb moment, this is likely to have occurred. If you can bring tools or learnings to them that make them respond in this manner, you are hitting a right note. They will feel good about this. They may even walk out with an extra spring in their step.
Make 'em go Wow	Through variety or the unexpected	Bring some twists and turns to your audience, making them feel as though they have been on an adventure, not so much sat and listened to a speech. Change up the different components of the piece and introduce some points that are unexpected leaving them changed by the whole experience.

We've covered a lot of ground, hope you made notes. Now it's your turn. Good luck!

Chapter Review:

In this chapter we have examined the following topics and learnings. We have:

I.   **Examined the power of a speaker.** How one speaker, with one speech, can have the impact of changing your life. For me it was hearing John Maxwell speak in Orlando Florida. *Who is it for you? Will you be that speaker for someone else?*

II. **Explored the 10 ways to engage your audience.** These included researching their industry, asking them questions directly or via a survey, buying them a coffee and conducting a brainstorming activity.

III. **Looked into 5 ways to leave an impact.** Whether it is use of humour, tugging at the heartstrings, making your audience feel better, learn something new or experience the unexpected. These are ways you can pack a POW into your presentation.

IV. **Learnt as a speaker, you are an Agent of CHANGE.** The opening of this chapter showed that before you can create change, you need to connect, offer value and design your speech with your audience in mind.

How can I apply this?

_____

_____

_____

_____

_____

_____

Chapter 2:

Expand Mindset

'We tell our ideas from our minds, but we sell our ideas from our hearts.'

Cavett Robert

Chapter 2: Expand Mindset

Do you like to stay fresh, relevant and in demand?

One way to stay fresh, new, relevant and in demand is to keep your mind expanded. In keeping the mind expanded you are open to new ideas, new interactions and new experiences. If you can not only maintain your own fresh perspective, but can expand the mindset of your audience, you are hitting the mark. Providing your content is smashing.

I'm going to go one step further here and say that to really extend your impact, why not be open to new people too. Many people 'think' they are open-minded and enjoy meeting people. I like to think that one of the ways to really observe this is to watch people when they are with their peers, or their friends, at, say, a convention. Some people are swept up in their circle of friends and that's where they stay. Others step beyond. They have time for their friends, those special people in their life, yet they are not aloof. They are approachable and happily open to new people and new conversations. I think this person is someone special, in the Superstar stakes. I say this because their field of view is wider than merely what is right in front of them and they are aware, self-aware. In fact, dare I suggest, I would call it being 'others aware'.

There is a great article that talks about how, when we identify that we need to improve ourselves, we tend to go for the building of our skills. We enrol in a course or seminar to develop our skillset. This is likely to result in a positive change within us, although we could go further. What we could do is to aim to broaden our mindset. Expand the boundaries of what we currently see as our reality.

A key point that I am building up to here is that sometimes in life we need to own up to the fact that 'we' or 'I' am not always right. Yes I know it's a shocking statement to some. Let's face it though, life has become more dynamic than that. I feel that people who are set in their ways are being left behind because when you limit your thinking, you limit your options. And you limit the possibilities that are always in front of you.

I remember during the many years I spent working in not-for-profit organisations, there were so many varied personalities involved. It surprised me the limits some people had on their thinking. For example, there was a common thinking (what I would call 'group think') around your level of experience being directly proportionate to your length of service. Now to me, I have never been a fan of the thinking that you need to have done something for 20+ years before you become worthy of being considered 'experienced'. Don't get me wrong, it is admirable that someone dedicates this kind of time to their cause, field of study or expertise. And to hold that up in praise is worthy too. I value that.

Having said this, I don't believe this is the only way possible to achieve expertise. Because, just as I have seen people with a lot of experience, sometimes it could mean they have 'done the time' and are now simply 'going through the motions'. I question, have they expanded themselves every step along the way, or have they merely repeated what they first learnt a multitude of times? I mean, just because a couple has been married for 20 years, does not always mean that they are necessarily happy. They may be cruising along not giving the relationship a lot of attention...

I worked for the Government, alongside military personnel, early in my career. Professional advancement occurred quite quickly and in doing so, colleagues and other people were naturally curious when they met me. It probably wasn't something they saw every day back then, a young civilian female in an executive level position. I can still hear their standard question: 'What's your background?' I've since noticed that this is pretty much a global question.   It represents a curiosity on the other person's part to enquire about what angle you are coming from and almost an underlying, unasked question as to whether you are worthy of their respect.

When asked this question, I would often gauge the reaction on the person asking's face when offering my response. In many instances, a short answer would require elaboration. It took me a while to realise that the person wanted to feel comfortable in themselves that I was performing the role I was. I learnt from this that the people who asked such a question were generally much older, baby boomers (if you believe these types of labels) and they needed to reconcile in their own mind that someone 'different' had joined the ranks. If they were happy with my reply, they felt at ease.

Here's another example of the necessity of expanding experience and mindset.

Case in point:

Jerry has been invited to speak to a group of young university graduates on the topic of project management. Jerry is 58 years old and he has been doing project management for thirty years. Jerry believes that he has a lot to offer the graduates and decides that his presentation will be all about his experience in project management and the projects he has worked on.

Bah-Bow. WRONG.

For this audience, Jerry needs to think differently. And make his presentation 'All About Audience'. It is more than that though. Jerry needs to expand his own knowledge first. Even though Jerry has amazing longevity in his field of work and within his industry, he needs to step beyond what he knows to reach this audience. Times have changed. Jerry needs to find some insights into this group of people, whether generation Y or the millennials, and understand what it is they will respond to. Because he hasn't had a lot of experience with them, he needs to expand his mindset before he can help his audience to do the same.

In what ways can I expand my mindset?

How about some of the following methods:

- <u>Read</u> - fill your mind with the right information. This doesn't include Facebook. Feed your brain. Read books (like this one - good start.). Find authors or thought leaders who expand your mind and enhance your thinking.

- <u>Learn</u> - be a keen student. If you can't afford (financially or space-wise) to stack the shelves of your living room with more books, visit your local library. Be open to learning new and different skills that will enhance your interest level as a person and that you can bring to your speaking. You'd be amazed at how new knowledge and skills just end up coming out when you are speaking, facilitating or training.

- <u>Grow</u> - step outside the comfort zone. Even though it sounds clichéd, putting yourself through new experiences, things you don't want to do but you know are good for you, can be real personal growth experiences. As Scott Harris says 'by its very nature, Growth is UNCOMFORTABLE!'

- <u>Teach</u> - when you speak, you are imparting an experience to another. Whether you connect with the terms 'teach' and 'teacher' or not, this is what you can and probably are doing. Without realising it.

- <u>Lead</u> - when you speak with your audience you lead them. A leader is a speaker. You need to have the moves, the actions and the thoughts of a leader. When you see the audience is not responding to you, part of your role is to read them and adapt accordingly. If you ignore the signs, they are likely to get worse. You will lose the audience and their respect along with it.

- <u>Mentor</u> - by being a mentor to someone you can learn so much yourself. Think back to when you were growing up. Who did you have as a mentor? You probably didn't call them that at the time, but you later realised they were. Because they offered you guidance and steered you in a good direction. They had you covered and they cared.

Agent of CHANGE

As a Speaker, I believe you are an Agent of Change. This is the first of the 7 Speaking Truths.

As an Agent of Change, you need to act as and be a Leader. To act as and be a leader, you need to have something more to give. Something exciting to be talking about. Cutting-edge ideas to share. If you are not ahead of the curve, your audience will sense this.

When you speak to your people, whether it is in a large theatre group or a small intimate workshop, they will walk away and in their mind's eye, they will be thinking one of two things about what they just heard:

1. Nothing different to what I already know, I will keep doing what I am doing. '**I don't need to change'**; or

2. I feel different having heard that. '**I want to change'.**

In my view, there is no middle ground. Your audience are either moving away from you (and your vision) or coming along for your ride. As a leader you want them coming with you. You are an Agent of CHANGE.

The word change can also be described as transformation or adaptation. Or my favourite, alteration. An interesting word, Alteration. There is the mediaeval Latin version - *alterationem*, though being from a French background, I prefer the French origin version - *Alteracion*. Sounds more exotic.

The origin of alteration is, unsurprisingly, linked to clothing. Last Tuesday, I took an item of clothing, it was a jacket, to my tailor, Lucy. I walked in to the shop and immediately I could smell the fabric of the different clothing types. I could hear the drilling of the sewing machines. Lucy took a look at my blue jacket, holding it up close to her eyes, inspecting it with amazing precision. She then examined the lining, like a detective trying to determine its history. Lucy looks at how clothing has been crafted. She has laser-like focus.

This is much like your audience. You'll have people who are already crafted, with set thoughts, already shaped. And then you are coming in as a speaker to alter them. This alteration should be a positive one that works in their favour.

When was the last time that you as a leader, took a laser-like focus to your people?

So EVERY time you speak to your audience, that's your time to help them. You want your audience to adapt to a new way. Even if it is in small, incremental steps.

Do you remember the song Imagine by John Lennon? (*I know, I know, how could you forget?*). It is SUCH a memorable, melodic song. From the start of the song the mood and tone is set with those low playing piano tones accompanying the really beautiful lyrics. Every time I hear that song, I try to stop what I am doing and listen to it. It is indeed a moving masterpiece.

Do you want to move your people when you speak?

You can.

When you are speaking to your people, think of them as your Tribe. Extensions of you. That's what they are. They are, in an organisational sense, extensions of your Vision. They are the arms and legs, and fingers and toes of your Vision. The question is, have they stopped moving, or are they just moving on the spot? Movement is important. Because 'movement leads to momentum'.

You need to make sure your message is crystal clear. You may have multiple messages. Don't have too many in the one speech, ideally have one. Depending on the length of the speech. If it is an hour long, maximum three. Make your message clear and repeat it several times.

Don't be afraid to mention an elephant in the room. Any big issue or hot topic that is looming and that relates to uncertainty. Such as the potential for a restructure. Be upfront and honest with your people. Respect them. One of the traits of High Performing Teams is not that they have fewer problems, they just address the ones they have.

Here's an action for you. Write down the top three changes you would like your people to make. List more if you have more of them. Ask yourself 'what do I wish my people would do, or do more of?' that would make my job easier and give us better results.

My top 3 changes for my people:

1. _____

2. _____

3. _____

I'd also like you to think about what you want your audience to think and feel by the end of your speech? 'Feel' as in what emotional state to do you want them to experience? Excited? Calm? Confident? Empowered?

_____

What would you like them to think? What logical mindset should they have?

_____

Take as long as you need. We can revisit these in our crafting and speechmaking activities.

As a Speaker, you are an Agent of CHANGE who can change the mindset of your audiences. Only after expanding your own mindset. Continuously.

Knowing self

One of the best things you can do to prepare yourself for more speaking is to get to know **You**. Yes, You. The one in the mirror. To understand you is to hone in on what brings you here, to this point in your life's journey. Even though we think we know ourselves, it is often only apparent when we are faced with a challenge or something that tests us.

A couple of years after joining the Australian Public Service in 1992, we had some consultants come in and do a Myer-Briggs assessment of us. If you are familiar with this methodology you will know that it is a personality evaluation. I thought it was so cool. Wow, a test that could reveal stuff about you?

What about you? Introvert or Extrovert? My partner, Philip, is convinced that I am an extrovert in disguise. I assure him I am not. I think he believes this because of the bright clothing I wear. Typical comment, coming from an extrovert!

Common definitions are that an extrovert gets their energy from being around others where an introvert derives their energy from being alone.

I prefer to refer to myself as *intro-steptive*. Yes I invented this term! So if you hear the kids using it out there on the streets, you know where it came from. Let me explain. A person who is *intro-steptive* is an introvert who likes (or at least pushes themselves towards) stepping outside their comfort zone. This is me. Although whether I like stepping outside the comfort zone - the jury is still out on that one - I often have to push myself to do it. Sometimes I would rather stay at home. Not to do nothing, but to be in a zone that I know to be productive and comfortable. Stepping outside can, however, lead to things magical and inspiring.

Continuous stepping out of the comfort zone has lead me to become better at what I do and improve my abilities, skills and knowledge. And as a person. The same goes for you and your speaking. What are you going to do to step outside your speaking comfort zone?

Comparing you to others

I don't recommend comparing you to others. In fact, you shouldn't. I don't believe that it serves you in a way that is either constructive or helpful. What I mean is that if you are, say, trying to make it as a talk show host, and you go comparing yourself to Oprah Winfrey, you may experience some feelings of, well, inferiority. Why? Because Oprah has a 20 year head start on you. That's why.

Does that mean you should stop right now and give it away? No way. By all means, look to Oprah and the masters for what they have achieved. Model parts of what you think makes the success happen. Then carve out your own unique path.

Ask for feedback from others too. I know that when I first started to get my speaking in the professional space, I had all kinds of advice. Which is good. One piece of advice was that you shouldn't name your company with words, you should keep it simple and use your own name.

For example, based on this advice, my website should be **www.annaperdriau.com.au**   rather   than **www.destinationexcellence.com.au** . For me, though, this doesn't quite fit the bill. There is nothing simple about Perdriau! Because I have a name that usually takes people at least a couple of attempts to pronounce correctly, and that's with coaching, let alone remembering how to spell it. Experience shows that learning how to pronounce 'purr-dree-O' takes several goes, coaching and more, and I don't want my audience to work that hard. So, for me, I had to get sassier about it. I wanted to hold on to the brand name 'Destination: Excellence!' while continuing to hone it and work it. I recommend seeking feedback, whether that is gaining direct feedback on a specific point, or tapping into networks for education. Feedback is a must.

Knowing others to know self

It amazes me how we human beings seem to be tuned-in to believing that we are <u>right</u>. I think it must be from when we were growing up and our parents knew best and we learnt this pattern of behaviour. Nowadays we don't see this as much where parents are the only ones who know best and what they say goes. Knowing yourself is the first step to being able to manoeuvre effectively around this planet we live on. First step here is: don't assume you are always in the right. Be open to being wrong. Listen to your dialogue. Do you wander around pointing out what others are doing wrong?

Hmmm, come on, be honest. We all need to eat a slice of humble pie from time to time. When was your last serving?

Mine was in July 2015. I had an opportunity to go overseas and I thought that I would just slink off and attend the NSA Convention in Washington DC. I didn't want to make a big deal of it, and being an introvert, I didn't want to post on social media every step of my journey. It was hard enough being away from my love, Philip. I just wanted to go and do my thing. Well. Those around me had other plans. I bumped into Sally at Brisbane airport. She posted online 'great to see you at Brisbane airport Anna, see you in the USA'.

I ended up bowing to the onslaught of messages and putting up a post about being overseas and what I was doing there. I guess I learnt a lesson. In these days of social media, there really is no such thing as privacy anymore.

On reflection though, of course my family and friends will be wanting to know what I'm doing and why and where I am. Because they care. And because they care, their instinct is to protect. And this is their way of showing that protection. I am lucky that I am loved.

Methods to know self better

How can you better get to know self? How about a good old fashioned SWOT analysis. You know - Strengths, Weaknesses, Opportunities and Threats. There's no fancy tool you need to purchase here, but draw up a table of four quadrants and put your dot points into each of the four squares. You'd be amazed at what comes out. Especially if you take your time to flesh it out with plenty of thoughts. Try it, you might be surprised.

Another method is to ask others. What others perceive of you can be different to how you see yourself. Doing online personality tests can also contribute. The more you know you, the better placed you are to understand others.

Understanding others

For the purpose of this section, we are going to think of your audience members similar to animal types. Why animal types? Because the animal kingdom is fascinating and we can learn so much from them of course. I'm not expecting that you will end up with fur envy or anything like that.

Let's look at the different samplings of audience member types you may come across, using animals as examples, what they are like and how you can best engage with them as audience members.

Table 3 - 5 Audience types represented as animals

#	Animal	Description	How to respond
1	Kangaroo	This audience member is the ideal. They love your content, they fully participate, has a great positive attitude, engages and takes interest. On top of that, this person goes onto social media and raves about you.	Treat like gold. Value this person. Make sure you check in with them and give them encouragement and plenty of positive feedback. Make sure they know you appreciate them in your words and actions.
2	Owl	A detail oriented type who likes to understand the material well. Studies. Often has lots of questions.	Feed their smarts and their desire to learn. Involve them. Let them delve and ask questions.
3	Galah	This audience member likes to laugh, joke around and have a great time. Usually an extrovert (though not necessarily).	Can be great participants and eager to volunteer in activities. Make sure you value them. If they are put down they could become distracting. Harness their fun energy by calling on them or making references

			to them in a positive manner.
4	Cockatoo	This audience member is distracting. They always want to question your content, interrupt or goof around.	This person needs to be managed. Otherwise they will take over and/or try and take the energy of the other audience members away from where you need them to be. Manage carefully.
5	Mouse	Quiet and smart. Generally is an introvert and is wanting to absorb the materials.	Involve them respectfully. Bring them out and include them. Don't make them do overly outrageous things. They may not be the first person to volunteer. This doesn't mean though that they aren't really into it.

*Note that most participants are a combination of the animals. For example a combination of a cockatoo and a mouse. Very enthusiastic yet quiet too.

The point of this table is for you to reflect on how you respond / manage. Be wary that you are not falling into the trap of giving the galah too much time and ensure that people like the mouse have their say too.

Chapter Review:

In this chapter we have examined the following topics and learnings. We have:

I.   **Explored the importance of keeping your mind expanded.** We saw the example of Jerry the project manager who had a speech to a group of people thirty years his junior but he did not think about his audience sufficiently when planning his speech to be able to connect with them. This can have disastrous consequences for a speaker as audience connection is key.

II.   **Ways to expand the mindset.** These included: Read (keep up your reading of books and the right sources of knowledge), Learn (continuous learning not only of new skills but of new knowledge in areas you wouldn't normally look into - step outside that zone), Grow (by its very nature, growth is uncomfortable, but keep pushing yourself to do it), Teach (others especially as a speaker we are constantly doing this and aim to do it in new and fresh ways), Lead (be a leader, set high standards and show the way it is done; don't stoop too low simply because everyone seems to be) and Mentor (identify those you can help, doesn't matter if they are not your family, offer to mentor others).

III. **Further reviewed being an Agent of CHANGE.**
As a speaker, your audience is walking away thinking
one of two things: 'I don't need to change', or 'yes, I
want to change.' We explored the origins of alteration
and how to ensure you can be a speaker who
stimulates positive change and empowers your
audience.

IV. **Examined self-awareness.** The importance of
understanding who you are as a person to be the best
speaker you can be. Are you an introvert or an
extrovert? How you relate with those around you, and
how you best perform, is important to know. This
then highlights the importance of self-awareness as
well as 'others awareness'.

V. **Discussed not comparing you with others.**
There is no value in comparing you with anyone else.
Although the temptation to do so may exist, there
really is only one you. As Oscar Wilde said 'Be
yourself. Everyone else is taken.'

VI. **Identified some audience types**. We looked at
the various animals that your audience members may
resemble. These were: Kangaroo (ideal), Galah (likes
a laugh), Owl (wise, into the detail), Cockatoo (can be
distracting) and Mouse (quiet yet really interested).

What about you?

_____

_____

_____

_____

_____

_____

_____

Chapter 3:

Extinguish Barriers

'When you talk, you give yourself away. You reveal your true character in a picture which is more true and realistic than anything an artist can do for you.'

Ralph C Smedley

Chapter 3: Extinguish Barriers

Why is public speaking a dirty word (or should that be two)?

I believe there are many reasons why people, especially adults, have blocked out public speaking from their mind, as being something they have no need or desire to do. Conversely, I meet a lot of people who believe it *would* be good for them to do it, but they have closed their mind to it. Until, that is, it becomes so urgent, so critical to their career progression, that they are backed into a corner. Only then do they seek assistance to improve their speaking. Let's delve further into why we still baulk at public speaking.

Flying across the USA

On a US Airways flight from Los Angeles to North Carolina, I got chatting to the lovely retired couple sitting next to me. Jenny asked me what I did....I told her that I am a public speaking coach and speaking stylist. 'Wow, where were you twenty years ago? I could have done with your help.' It turns out that Jenny had spent her life as a schoolteacher, confiding 'I was fine when it came to being at the front of the room with my school kids. But you ask me to present to my peers and that's a whole other ballgame. I was asked to present at a convention once and never did it again.' Gosh. Jenny's experience had been so isolating and traumatic that she closed off to all future possibility of speaking outside of her classroom. Jenny clearly still went on to have an enriching career, though even she admitted it would have been good to not have had to stop it there.

It's as though the trauma of not knowing how is crippling us people. Let's change this right now. And then continue to do so. Because the human race needs leaders now more than ever.

Jenny's story had me realising that her reference to public speaking was so common. I recognised that there are a number of reasons for people not pursuing public speaking. Reasons beyond simply 'not wanting to'. Jenny's experience led me to devise a top 9 (and a bonus +1) reasons why, as adults, we don't pursue public speaking as a worthy activity beneficial to ourselves and others. I'll share my conclusions with you here:

Table 4 - Top 9 (+1 bonus) Countdown for reasons why adults don't do Public Speaking:

9	Society	Society conditions us to fear public speaking. The first words associated with public speaking are 'fear', 'nerves', 'sweaty palms' etc. These messages are entered into our head before we even have a chance to try it out for ourselves.

8	People	Other people condition us to be afraid of public speaking - again before we even have a chance to experience it. They do this by making negative comments about it. This is because they harbour fear of it, and they can pass their hang-up on to us. Without realising they are doing it.
7	It's not easy	Nothing is easy when we don't know how. Ok, maybe that's not entirely true. There may be some things we can figure out for ourselves and find it easy to do so. For example, understanding how to turn a light switch on might be easy. Knowing how to read your audience, what to say and how to engage them.....that takes time and skills. So until these skills are learned, experienced and practiced, they are not so easy. This is why adults don't speak. It's too difficult.
6	We are not practiced	We don't know how. Therefore we are fearful. We want to know how to do something and be practiced at it before really wanting to do it. Public speaking is one of those things that being practiced in, helps a whole lot.
5	Bad experience	Typically, something happened as a kid when you stood up in class for show and tell. All the other kids laughed at you, even though what you said wasn't meant to be funny, and you haven't been the same since. Somewhere deep down in your psyche you recorded that as a definitely bad experience and your mind learnt not to put

		yourself in that type of danger again. Oh yes, the bad experience category.
4	No-one told us we 'could'	No-one tapped you on the shoulder and said 'hey you'd be great at this. Let me take you by the hand and wave my magic wand and before you know it, you'll be a Star.' What, you mean that never happened to you? Oh diddums. Guess what? That never happens to any of us. Sure we come across people who believe in us along the way, those who become Mentors in our life and careers. But really - stop expecting others to believe in you. You believe in You. I believe in You. YOU CAN DO THIS.
3	We're actively avoiding it	Just like the way you ignored your ex-boyfriend or girlfriend when you saw them at a party back in college. As adults some of us are actively, and I mean going out of our way, to avoid having to give a speech. Stop this. Help is here. You don't have to feel this way again.
2	We think it's for 'other people'	We see people speaking on the microphone and at the front of the room and we think: 'oh I could never do THAT. That's for other people. That's for confident people.' Ok, let's turn around this thinking to be 'hey I'd like to do THAT. I can do THAT.' Yes, public speaking is most certainly for You.

1	We lack confidence	Feeling modest? Ditch it. Not sure if it's 'for you'. Rubbish. Speaking is for you. You have a story. You have a message. You have people to serve. Stop being so insular with your thinking. Be confident and serve.
+1	It's not COOL.	We like to 'do lunch'. We don't like to 'do' public speaking. In other words, we don't realise the value that public speaking has. Thus we need to switch on the light. The time to do this is now.

What are the things holding you back from being the speaker that you know you can be?

Money, time, support... the list goes on. There is always something getting in the way of things we want to do. Think of these as part of the challenge.

'Money doesn't grow on trees'. You have probably heard this old saying. Again, probably another 'parentism' used by mums and dads across the globe when confronted with a certain request from their children. 'Daddy, I want one.' 'Not right now Timmy. We can't afford that right now. Remember what Daddy said before, *(here it comes, wait for it, here it comes...)* money doesn't grow on trees.'

Well-intentioned parents around the globe use this line (at least, they used to) for various reasons: instilling the right values in their kids, teaching them to value their finances, bringing a dose of reality to the forefront, and for myriad other reasons (like keeping their child at bay and from having to make that purchase).

The Countdown demonstrates why adults don't do public speaking. It is important that we acknowledge these points and examine how we can move beyond them. Let's consider some strategies we can employ to combat each one of the top 9 (+1) reasons.

I believe that these negative reasons can be group into three different categories, as follows:

1. <u>Other people (group)</u> - a group of people, other than you, who are impacting how you feel, think or behave regarding public speaking.

2. <u>Other people (singular)</u> - a person who on their own impacts how you feel, think or behave concerning public speaking.

3. <u>You</u> - your own self, your inner voice and how you see You and what you can or cannot do, in relation to public speaking.

Here are some strategies I believe you can employ to address each of these three categories of people.

Activity

Before examining these strategies though, I suggest that you write down on a piece of paper all of the great things about you including:

- qualifications

- education level

- personality traits

- attitude

- special qualities (that make you unique)

<u>Note</u>: *Don't stop until you've listed at LEAST 30 points. All good ones too.*

After completing your list, take a look at it. Look at all of your great qualities - there is an audience out there for you.

Once you've done this, you can move on to the Strategies Table.

Table 5 – Strategies to help get you ready to take on public speaking (using the Countdown results)

#	Reasons for not doing public speaking	Category falls into (1, 2 or 3)	Strategies to adopt
1	Society made me feel I couldn't or shouldn't. Many people commented, no one told me I could / should.	Other people (group)	Start to develop a listening ear for the types of broad generalisations you hear coming from people in groups or in society that can be damaging to the self-esteem of others. Listen out for examples of this. Take a mental note of this happening. Even jot it down in your notebook. Later have a reflection on this and see how 'we' as humans can improve the situation. How can we learn from our mistakes and turn things around for the positive.
2	I had a bad experience once. No one told me I could / should / would	Other people (single)	No one has the right to take your hopes and dreams away from you. If you have someone in your life whom you care about, but who does not believe that you can achieve great things, such as taking the step into speaking, then

	be any good at it. I always thought it was for 'other people'.		you should have an open dialogue with them. Let the person know how you feel honestly. If the person you believe put you off speaking is not someone you care about or for, then just remove that memory. Or, use it to spur you on.
3	It's not easy. I'm not practiced. I've been actively avoiding it. I think it is for others. I have a lack of confidence in it. It's not COOL.	'You' In this case, you are your own worst enemy. You need to re-introduce yourself to you, and become best friends. And enjoy it :-)	Start with a positive dialogue with yourself. Develop standard daily 'affirmations' for yourself in relation to public speaking and speak them to yourself - aloud. For example, 'I am a great public speaker who has a lot of value to add to my audience'. Say this to yourself daily in the mirror and really sound as though you mean it. Do mean it.

Note: *Even though points 1 and 2 discuss how it was external factors that stopped adults from public speaking, ultimately it always comes back to you to determine what you make happen. In other words, even if someone or a group of 'someones' tells you that you can't, or you shouldn't, or you are not good enough, you can build your confidence to be so robust that you know you CAN do anything you set your mind to.*

Making it work in your favour

How is it that successful people make 'it' work? In this case, 'it' is an all-inclusive term for anything and everything. Successful people make it work for them. *How does this magic happen?* By thinking differently. By challenging assumptions. And by having courage. *Courage?* Yes, by having the courage to stand up to well-meaning friends and family who love you dearly. Let me explain. Family and friends love you dearly. But they can be time stealers, so watch out. Family thinks nothing of sitting around chatting for hours on end. *Let's face it though, who has time to do that anymore?* Time is the most precious thing we have. *With the magic 168 hours we each have per week, how many people do you know who are really conscious of how they use it?*

I'm not saying don't spend time with those people you love. No siree. I am saying that time spent with anyone should be time that is rationed. We set times for meetings in business. Why wouldn't we do the same in our personal life? Even though, of course, family are more important and are always going to need you at certain times, and you may not have scheduled that in.

Let's do a quick check of you. *What are the things that are not serving you but which you are spending time on?* For example, two of the biggest time stealers out there are television and the World Wide Web. Especially Facebook.

I'm not saying don't spend time doing things you enjoy. Certainly not. I'm highlighting that you should be conscious of what you are doing.

Rearranging priorities

We all get into habits. They form. We get comfortable. How about questioning what these habits are. To do this you can look into how much time you are spending on various activities. For example, over the course of a typical week, how many hours do you spend (a) sleeping, (b) at work, (c) with family, (d) exercising, (e) on hobbies, (f) surfing the web, (g) watching tv, and (h) other.

Name (at least) one thing that you could reduce time on:

_____

Then commit to making a change. You could replace with time to work on your speaking.

Nerves

Why is it that when we're chatting with our best friend, we sound casual, charming and fun, yet put us in front of an audience and we turn into a knocked-kneed, bumbling mess?

It's that little thing called nerves. Those little critters JUMP out and scare us, don't they?

(Note: see also Chapter 7 - entice vocally)

Table 6 - Techniques to manage your nerves before speaking

#	Technique	Details
1	Centre You	Find a moment to gather self. Some people like to be alone before they speak whereas others draw strength from being around people. Find what works for you. It may be a quiet meditation time. Or one minute of 'power centring'.
2	Breathing	Ten minutes before you speak (or even earlier) you can experience the rush of adrenaline into your body. If not treated the right way, and harnessed, that adrenaline could work against you. In order to prepare your autonomic nervous system (ANS) start to do slow breathing (up to 10 seconds in and out through the nose) before you go on.
3	Vocal Warm-ups	Your vocal warm-up routine should include breathing from the diaphragm.

| 4 | Organs of Articulation warm-ups | Run through the Organs of Articulations warm-ups listed in this book. This will loosen up your organs so that you don't get tongue tied when you speak. |
| 5 | SMILE. | Before you think 'that's sounds silly', when you smile, it releases happy chemicals within you and causes you to relax. (Your brain doesn't know the difference remember.). Find someone who looks friendly and greet them, shake hands and smile. If you can have a laugh with them, you'll feel even better. |

Chapter Review:

In this chapter, by working through the various topics and learnings, we have:

I.   **Explored the nervousness associated with public speaking.** We met Jenny from the USA who had been a schoolteacher yet avoided public speaking outside the classroom. We discovered how this is a common story.

II.   **Looked at the countdown** for the top 9 (+1) reasons why adults don't do public speaking. Reasons such as not being encouraged to, because it's not easy, we think it's for 'other people' and there can be a perception that public speaking is 'not cool'.

III. **Asked you the question 'what is stopping you from public speaking?'** We explored that there are always a range of reasons for not pursuing something we want to do, and there are pathways to make it happen too. Conducted an exercise where you reviewed the activities on which you spend your time during a typical week and identifying options where you can seek to reduce certain activities and replace them with speaking time. Making it work in your favour.

IV.   **Highlighted the three different categories** stopping people from pursuing, and reasons they think are holding them back from, public speaking.   A combination of other people (groups and single) and yourself.

V.   **Examined strategies on how to make it work.** This is to combat all of the reasons outlined in the Countdown 9 (+1). This is all about making it work for you.

VI.   **Techniques to manage your nerves.** What you can do to manage the nerves before speaking, from breathing to vocal warm-ups, to preparation.

What about you?

_____

_____

_____

_____

_____

_____

Chapter 4:

Exude Confidence

'The audience wants you present,
not perfect.'

Darren LaCroix

Chapter 4: Exude Confidence

Confidence. We know it when we see it. I'll bet you can name someone who represents complete confidence. Have a think about it.

When I think of confidence, I think of the character played by Leonardo DiCaprio, Mr Gatsby, in the movie The Great Gatsby. Every move he made was confident. His walk, his talk, his smile, his demeanour. There was nothing he couldn't handle, everything was taken care of down to the tiniest of detail.

To me, he was Mr Confident.

Who is your confidence role model?

_____

_____

(Note: the editor of this book prefers Robert Redford as a better example for Mr Gatsby.)

Even though confidence seems to be an elusive quality reserved for some, I believe confidence can be broken down into its key components, worked on and improved upon.

Here's how I break down confidence. It's the 4 Ps to Confidence Creation:

P #1 – Presentation

The first of the four Ps is Presentation. In other words, Present You.

The way that you present yourself to the world matters. From your first decisions of the day regarding what to wear through to how you 'show up' on the day.

In Chapter 6 (Energise) we will be discussing the significance of appearance. Thus, it is important that you look the part of the successful person you want to portray.

This is one piece of the presentation jigsaw.

Another part is the way that you have it all 'together'. You are organised and you are clean, tidy and present well.

You may be thinking, '*but Anna, I'm no fashionista*'.

That's fine, you don't need to be. There are many people to help you. There are people you can employ to make you look good. Who know exactly what will work with your body type, shape, face, height, width and personality. Alternatively there are free resources out there to help you with your image. Online videos to help with the skills to recognise which colour scheme works for you (are you best matched with winter, summer, spring or autumn colours?) and easily accessible. Get to know the colours that suit you. You can sometimes tell these anyway because you wear something that people compliment you on or say 'you look great today.'

Remember that image is brand. It's a fun discovery activity.

P #2 – Projection

The second of the four Ps is Projection. This is all about how YOU project to the world.

What this means is, every little detail of your body language: your walk, talk, posture, breathing, tone, words and actions. How composed you are. Whether what you say matches your actions. Congruency is key.

Most importantly, don't forget to SMILE.

P #3 – Positivity

The third of the four Ps is Positivity.

I've always been a fan of people watching. Not only for how people walk or chat to each other in public, but also I like to see how people respond to conflict situations. Even at the most minute level.

Case in point:

It was 3:45am at the Dulles airport, in Washington DC. I had checked in my suitcase and went through to the security screening area where I found a very long waiting line. I mean looongggg.

I was somewhat shocked to find such a long line. I think in my mind I had thought, 'It's early morning, who else would be crazy enough to be up at this time?' On reflection, it occurred to me that it was probably entirely normal that there would be so many people waiting in the line at this time of day. It was a major airport and this is a great time of day to travel. When you travel early, you get to your destination early. As the old saying goes, the early bird catches the worm. Well that, and we all probably got a better deal because of the time of day.

My only concern was that I only had about half an hour before my flight was due to board. I didn't want to be late, but didn't know how fast or slow this lane was moving either.

Once I had resolved in my mind that I just needed to stay alert to the time, I decided not to panic. I wanted to trust that this situation would be ok and that the queue was moving at a suitable pace.

I noticed that the responses of other people as they had to join the queue were the same. Some people verbalised it.

'Oh my gosh.' Others said the same thing but in their facial expression. Their eyes would go very wide.

One man, who was two places behind me in the line, had an altogether different response.

'Oh my goodness.' he exclaimed. Then he started pacing on the spot almost like a small child who needed to go to the bathroom urgently. He looked at his phone. He looked up at the screen searching for answers. Clearly his flight was boarding soon and he was panicked by the sight of the long line.

I'm not saying that his response was right or wrong, I just know that when you get upset, it takes up a lot of energy. And this man was burning it up. It's a good thing it was morning time when you (theoretically) have energy. I was worried he was about to burst.

He was huffing and puffing. He kept repeating the same phrase 'Oh my goodness'. Then he went up to one of the airport staff and asked her a question. Clearly her answer was to recommend staying in the line. But she had good news - there were two lines. What looked like a mass of people was in fact two orderly lines. He immediately jumped into the shorter of the two lines and his body language changed. He relaxed. It was the positive news that had his mind put at ease.

The positive news resulted in an amazing change in his demeanour.

So if you surround yourself with positive news, can this result in you being more positive?

In short, yes.

Attitude

Your attitude really does make a difference. And it doesn't take a lot of effort. Because it all starts in the mind. And what happens in the mind can be shaped.

If your response to things that happen is a positive one, you are more likely to see the hope that will move you forward, as opposed to the obstacles that could hold you back.

What I'm getting at here is not that you need to turn into Mary Poppins and see the world only in glowing terms and behave accordingly, but that you can be in control of your reactions. And your reactions to date may have been holding you back.

Every word that comes from your mouth can shape the automatic response you have. And this is all to do with what is happening in your mind.

This is where the work of Dr Albert Ellis is really fascinating. Dr Albert Ellis was an American psychologist who developed Rational Emotive Behavior Therapy, REBT. He is considered one of the world's most influential psychotherapists.   Over the course of his decades-long career, Dr Ellis wrote more than 60 books and founded the Albert Ellis Institute. He helped people with everything from how to quit smoking, communicate more effectively and improve their sexual and personal relations.

In the 1950s Dr Ellis' invented R.E.B.T. Here is an excerpt about REBT from www.rebtnetwork.org illustrating how it works:

Rational Emotive Behavior Therapy

REBT is based on the premise that whenever we become upset, it is not the events taking place in our lives that upset us; it is the beliefs that we hold that cause us to become depressed, anxious, enraged, etc. The idea that our beliefs upset us was first articulated by Epictetus around 2,000 years ago: '*Men are disturbed not by events, but by the views which they take of them.*'

The ABC Model

Albert Ellis and REBT posit that our reaction to having our goals blocked (or even the possibility of having them blocked) is determined by our beliefs. To illustrate this, Dr. Ellis developed a simple ABC format to teach people how their beliefs cause their emotional and behavioral responses:

A. Something happens.

B. You have a belief about the situation.

C. You have an emotional reaction to the belief.

For example:

A. Your employer falsely accuses you of taking money from her purse and threatens to fire you.

B. You believe, 'She has no right to accuse me. She's a bitch.'

C. You feel angry.

If you had held a different belief, your emotional response would have been different:

A. Your employer falsely accuses you of taking money from her purse and threatens to fire you.

B. You believe, 'I must not lose my job. That would be unbearable.'

C. You feel anxious.

The ABC model shows that **A** does not cause **C**. It is **B** that causes **C**. In the first example, it is not your employer's false accusation and threat that make you angry; it is your belief that she has no right to accuse you, and that she is a bitch. In the second example, it is not her accusation and threat that make you anxious; it is the belief that you must not lose your job, and that losing your job would be unbearable.

Dr Ellis believes that you can control your reactions to what has happened to you through addressing your thoughts and how you hold a set of beliefs at B.

In an instant you can change your automatic instincts and avoid reacting in the same way you've always done. Before answering or countering, you can take the briefest moment to pause, consider and only then respond.

How does the work by Dr Ellis relate to confidence?

Dr Ellis' work proves that to be confident doesn't mean that everything is going to go your way all of the time. And that when it does not, there is a set of beliefs we may hold about ourselves, and about others, preventing us from responding in a completely unemotive manner. As a speaker, you need to be open to change, able to adapt to evolving circumstances. If you can take them in your stride and do not expect unrealistically that everything is going to roll in your favour 100% of the time, then you will be better placed not to over-react emotionally to events. You can accept them and move with grace through any change that comes your way.

As Dr Ellis' work goes on to address, you should aim to hold unconditional self-acceptance, unconditional other-acceptance and unconditional life acceptance. All of these revolve around acceptance that a human being is not perfect, others will not treat you fairly all of the time and that I as a human being am no more or no less worthy than another human being.

Confidence occurs as much off the stage as it does on stage. Confidence is about more than mere bravado. Confidence is not ego. This applies also to comments you make about your experience at the event. If you make comments that are negative about the event or your experience of the event to people in passing, this can reflect negatively upon you. Always be professional in your dealings and comments about events you speak at. You never know who those comments might be passed on to. You'll want to build and gain your reputation in the right way, with integrity from the start.

Where do you sit on the confidence spectrum?

|_____|

Low self-image   Confident   Ego driven

High Performance Thinking

Another reference point here is High Performance Thinking expert, Eric Pace, an Australian entrepreneur, trainer and leader.

Eric talks about his upbringing, where his father worked on the railways, and of growing up and starting in the same industry, earning a university degree and becoming a railway engineer.

He mentions how he'd never really thought about doing anything different.   Until he got into reading self-development books and expanded his mind.

After more than 20 years studying this topic, Eric now runs two-day seminars on high performance thinking.   An exceptional trainer, Eric has the gift of transforming peoples' lives. Including mine.

I highly recommend you look at Eric's work. He's the most engrossing trainer I have experienced. Among the world's best.

Check him out at: highperformancethinking.com.au

P #4 – Presence

The fourth of the four Ps is Presence.

My reference to Presence here is all about being present. Your audience will believe you more when they believe you are 100% with them. And for them. You can still have their attention without 100% presence, but you won't have the same impact.

What I mean is, the difference between someone who is not completely present compared to one who's 100% focused on you. Let's call person 1 Terry and person 2 Sam:

Terry turns up early and is organised. Sets the room up. Makes sure you have all you need. Terry gives all his attention to you during the session. Delivers a great presentation or seminar. Makes you feel educated, inspired, uplifted. Terry has an offer. Overall, a worthwhile event.

Sam engages you via social media by creating excitement about the upcoming speech. This probably involves asking questions to get to know you (and your needs) better as an audience member. Turns up early, and is organised. Sets the room up. Makes sure you have all you need. Sam gives all his attention to you during the session and in-between the sessions. Delivers a great presentation or seminar. Makes you feel educated, inspired, uplifted. Sam has an offer. Follows up afterwards. Overall, an excellent experience.

So what is the difference? Terry does everything that makes a great experience. Sam however, goes further and takes engagement to a new level. Sam starts engaging with you before the event. Sam is thinking about how to delight you. Sam goes beyond the event itself.

I hear you thinking 'Anna, but what if I have things going on in my life that need my attention?....I don't have time to do all that extra engagement.'

Yes, I hear you. There is always so much going on and we have people and other things that need us. What I'm saying is that the more you give to your audience, the more you will gain.

Terry gives a great presentation. Terry gets great results. Sam's approach takes it a step beyond. Eventually Sam's approach will be the norm. What now seems extra effort will become the effortless approach in the future. So start now and get ahead of the curve.

The following table summarises the 4 Ps to confidence creation:

Table 7 – Summary of the 4 Ps to Confidence Creation

#	Confidence attribute	Details
1	Presentation - Present well	• Grooming • No distractions • Clean, tidy, well presented • Variety • Effort. • SMILE!

2	Projection
	
	- Project yourself
		• Body language
		   - Posture
		   - Walk
		   - Breathing
		   - Gestures
		• SMILE!

3	Positivity - Be Positive	• Attitude • Regardless of subject • Watch your reactions • Pause and think

		• Frame comments • See opportunity • SMILE!
4	Presence - Be Present	• Awake and alert • Dedicated to audience • Focused on outcome • Listen (actively) • Show interest • SMILE!

* Don't forget to smile.

Back to your confidence role model. *Did you identify that person?*

Consider how your 'Mr Gatsby' applies the 4 Ps to confidence. Including how they present themselves to the world. Consider how it is that they put themselves together to look that way. What it is that they do that is unique.

Also, how is their projection? How do they show their genuine intention through their body language and gestures?

How do they respond to the situations? Are they always positive in the way they respond?

Are they present with those around them? Do they give their full attention to those around them?

Maybe you know various confidence role models. There could be a role model who is exceptional at presenting themselves. Another role model could be for giving full attention to those around them. Like me, your role models could be a character, celebrity or movie star.

Your Speaking Style

What's a Speaking Style and why do I need one?

A 'Speaking Style' is the signature look and feel of you as a speaker, seen from the audience's perspective.

Put simply, if the audience were to describe three words they think of and remember having experienced you speak. Your personal qualities. Your persona as speaker. Ask yourself, 'as a speaker, am I typically energetic, entertaining, thought provoking, intellectual'?

Every time you speak you want to be an agent of change. To be an agent of change is the first of the 7 Speaking Truths. What you want to achieve is that by the time they leave having seen, heard and felt you speak, they have been moved to make a change.

How do I uncover my Speaking Style?

Here's how to find your Speaking Style in 3 easy steps:

Step 1 - Brainstorm

Brainstorm. Write a list of 30 qualities about yourself. Make sure you write down at least 30, no less. If you push to write down 30, you will be sure to have a great cross section of ideas from which to draw for step 2. Pushing past the comfort list level will enable you to be more creative, revealing real gems that wouldn't normally have surfaced.

Step 2 - Select

Taking your list of 30 personal qualities, go through and select the top 3 words that truly represent the style you want your audience to think of you. What are those words you want to be remembered for? Lock them in.

Step 3 - Embody

Take these three qualities and project them in your speech. 'Be' these qualities consistently when speaking and connecting with your audience. Bring them out in a way that celebrates them. Own them. Include them in your speaker introduction. Have them become your Speaking Style.

It is important to note here that in picking three identity words and embracing them in your performance and presentation, this is not to say that you won't have other qualities you bring out as needed. These are the 3 predominant ones.

Observe the learnings from this chapter including how to achieve levels of excellence and model what you do upon great examples and finding your Speaking Style.

My notes:

_____

_____

_____

_____

Chapter Review:

In this chapter we have examined the following topics and learnings:

I.   **Explored the notion of a confidence role model.** Looked into who that person or character may be for you, e.g. Mr Gatsby. Is there someone you know or have seen who embodies confidence for you? Identify this person and have him / her as your guide, your shining light for confidence.

II. **Learnt the 4 Ps to Confidence Creation.** (1) Presentation, and presenting you to the world, is the first step to how you are perceived and received. (2) Projection and how you hold yourself, your movement, body language and gesturing forms important communication tools. (3) Positive attitude is key to how you respond to all that happens to you (also refer to the info on Dr Albert Ellis). (4) Presence is about being 100% focused on your audience and being present with them. Together, these four steps are key to creating your own confidence.

III. **Discovered what makes up your Speaking Style.** Your unique qualities, your personality and special traits make up your speaking style. Identify the top three traits you bring to your speaking and then bring them out on stage. For example, you may have serious, analytical and dry witted as your three. We looked at the brainstorm activity to show what you can do to uncover what these qualities are for you.

IV.   Been reminded of the importance to....SMILE!

What about you?

_____

_____

_____

_____

_____

_____

Spectacular yet simple structure

Chapter 5:

Easy Structuring

'Don't forget the divinity
of simplicity.'

Cavett Robert

Chapter 5: Easy Structuring

You've poured a cup of tea and sat down to write your speech. Now STOP.

Before you start 'writing' your speech, whether your preferred method is typing, handwriting or dictating, I highly recommend conducting an 'audience analysis'. Laying the foundation for a successful audience engagement.

You can start by asking two key questions:

Who is my audience?

Your message means nothing if it is centred around you alone. This step is to understand what kind of individuals make up this grouping of people. It is to understand what they value, what motivates them and what things are important to them. Again, I hear you cry 'but Anna, they are a diverse group of people with many differences.' That's ok. Focus on what makes them the same. Consider what the common kernels are.

What is their need?

If these two questions are not asked before you start your speech, it will be a matter of you crafting your speech based on what you want to say.

Doing this exercise of asking those two questions is you conducting what I like to call your 'audience audit'. The word 'audit' might not be the sexiest word around but hey, let's give it a new image. Let's call it...a 'curiosity crosscheck'.

If you don't perform a curiosity crosscheck on your audience, you are going to craft your content from one angle, your angle, rather than the angle of what your audience needs.

Why is this important?

The approach most people have when they sit down to prepare their speech is to simply consider what they know about a topic. It is important to consider what key part of that knowledge will be of use and then frame it in a simple, memorable way for your audience.

Here are the four easy steps to conduct an audience analysis:

4 EASY STEPS TO CONDUCT AN AUDIENCE ANALYSIS

- <u>Identify - who are they?</u> What is it that binds this audience? This may be very specific reason, e.g. tax accountants, criminal lawyers or federal politicians. Or they may be a broader audience, e.g. people interested in wealth building, public speaking or arts and crafts. As a discrete group, identify who they are and give their group a name.

- <u>Identify - what are their traits?</u> List what it is that makes them similar within that group. What are their common attributes, such as age range (25-35), where they live, education level etc.? You can list as many as you want here. This is an opportunity to build a profile of what they are like.

- <u>Identify - how do they think?</u> Specifically, identify the way they think as a group in terms of statements they may say, such as their 'group think' - the thoughts / comments / mindset that are common to them as an audience. What thoughts, pre-conceptions and biases are likely to be running through their collective mind? For example, an audience of politicians at a public speaking presentation may think 'we already know how to speak, we speak all the time' as well as 'we are busy so don't waste our time' and 'this better be good'.

- <u>Ask 'how can I help them?'</u> You have done an identification at steps 1 -3, and you have analysed the profile of your audience. Now that you understand their frame of reference, from here ask yourself how you can match what their needs are (as fleshed out at step 3) with the knowledge and skills you have. Thus, to illustrate this in an equation would be:

KNOWLEDGE   +   NEEDS   =   VALUE

(yours)   (theirs)   (you can bring them)

To explain this, your total knowledge minus their specific needs in relation to your topic equals a very specific portion of what they need from you. Therefore, your total knowledge minus their specific needs equals the value you can add to this audience. Yay.

Here is a table summary of the easy steps to conduct your audience analysis:

1. Identify who they are?	2. Identify what are their traits?	3. How do they think?	4. How can I help them?

In Summary, the most important thing to do in any speech is to add value to your audience. These four easy steps can allow you to do a quick audience analysis so that you understand them before you decide how you are going to engage them with your phenomenal presentation.

If you find that you don't know too much about your audience as yet, you know that there are ways of finding out more about them. You can contact the event planner / organiser. You can see if there is a way for you to conduct a survey or speak with them directly. More about this is covered elsewhere in this book. Either way, you don't need to go in to your presentation with the feeling that you don't know anything about your audience. That would be so sad indeed.

How do I start my presentation?

In an engaging manner.   Yes? This really is the most important thing for you to do. You can use some of the following ways, though I'm confident you can be more creative than this.   I think you can go beyond what is expected.   Because the last thing you want to do is to be..........PREDICTABLE. In fact let's ban predictability as well as boring shall we? Yes? Done.   No further correspondence shall be entered into on that point.

Here are some types of speech opening you may like to consider:

Table 8 – Six Speech Openings – Options

1	Statistic	If you are going to start with a statistic, don't make it one that everyone has already heard. Make it unique. 'The woolley tree frog is the only frog in the world who grows wool and he can survive any cold climate. How are you like the woolley tree frog?' (*Note this is an example only, not a fact.*)
2	Story	No this is not 'Once upon a time there lived a little girl who called herself Little Red Riding Hood'. It's more like 'Red Riding Hood, watch out, look behind you....' With this as an opening line, the drama is created. You're already into the scene. The audience knows that something is about to happen and it could have serious consequences.

3	Show	You could start with a video on your topic that has music, movement, motion and is captivating. It could feature you or it could feature others. It must have a point, be meaningful and add to your presentation. If done well, this can be a lively entrance into your topic.*
4	Song	Is there a song that you could sing? Not everyone who speaks can be blessed with a singing voice, but there could be a reason for you breaking into song either at the start of or during the speech. You might use a well-known tune with your own, self-penned lyrics. This could be really engaging.
5	Share poem	This could be a poem you wrote: '*Almost 3,000 years ago, public speaking had folks like Plato. There was also a woman in the mix, when it came to brains, she hit 'em for six.*' Just using a sample of one of my own. Now if poetry is not your thing, go with what is, what works for you. No harm in trying new things either.
6	Starting Question	Ask a question of your audience. As already discussed, make it a relevant question and make sure there is a reason for asking it. Make the replies meld into your content to show you've done something with the information, rather than just used it as a novelty.

* Note that if you are going to use songs or clips from movies always check out the copyright and whether you need to pay a royalty to use them.

What is most important about your opening is that it engages. You want to create a positive energy and you want the audience to be listening and more so, paying attention to what is happening next. Or wondering what will come next.

Case in point:

I had the privilege to be a speaker at an ANZAC Tribute Event. The event marked the centenary of the start of World War I and honoured the fallen servicemen and women who'd sacrificed their lives in the conflict. I was sharing the stage with speakers holding a variety of awards and decorations. Although I was a decorated, award-winning leader, the lady who invited me to participate, Prema, had never seen me deliver a speech that wasn't an educational style speech.

I wanted to do a great speech. I particularly wanted to honour the Australian Army Nurses. I told the story in the first person as Sister Elsie Tranter (whose diary I had read) and even wore the outfit of a WWI nurse. My opening included reciting a poem I had memorised, by a South African woman who wrote it about the Australian soldiers. These women went to War and put themselves in danger, but on their return were treated like second class citizens.

Because females weren't recognised in 1918. I put more effort into this speech than any other I had ever created. I loved it.

The night was a huge success. A day later I received a testimonial from one of the other speakers. She was a highly respected and accomplished speaker and when I read what she said about me, I felt humbled. 'Anna has a flair for the unexpected.' She had seen something in me that no one else had.

My fellow speaker gave me a gift that night. She encouraged me to be me. And be more me. She helped me realise that I was on a track. And for that, I am eternally grateful.

Sometimes I think that we can be seeking the permission to be ourselves. As a speaker though, YOU is what makes you unique and not blend in to the others. So part of our journey as a speaker is to bring out the uniqueness in ME.

What's the main thing about you that makes you different as a speaker?

Speech content

These are your lessons you will leave with your audience. Those enduring life lessons you have absorbed that you know can benefit them. You know, those ones you learnt the hard way?

A general rule of thumb is to have one message per ten minutes of content. By all means use this as a guide, though do what works for you. You cannot force yourself to come up with a particular message if it doesn't make sense to do so. The key thing is to make sure your audience knows why they are doing what they are doing, in the case of an activity. Or, if it is a content piece, that you have your foundational phrase in there. Your core message that will leave them with a lasting impression. That central message that has meaning and that will endure throughout the ages. That's the aim.

Let's play with an hour long session here. You could break it down as follows:

Table 9 - Keynote session breakdown - Sample

Introduction	15 mins	Opening interaction question
		Story to engage
		Foundation Phrase
		Review / Transition to Block 1
Block 1	10 mins	Activity
		Report back
		Discussion
		Review / Transition to Block 2
Block 2	10 mins	Activity
		Report back
		Discussion
		Review / Transition to Block 3
Block 3	10 mins	Story to engage
		Foundational Phrase
		Review / Reflections
Summary	15 mins	Summarise
		Review
		Call to Action

It depends on your content and the activities you have planned as to whether you are able to fit in three Blocks. You may only need two.

Transitions and Speech Design

Transitions are a necessary tool for effective speech rhythm and flow. A transition is defined in the Collins dictionary as: 'change or passage from one state or stage to another'. In the context of music, transitions are about modulation, moving from one key to another, or bridging divisions in a composition.

In your speech, a transition is a link. When you take a step back and look at your speech from a macro perspective, you should be able to pick out the common thread running through it. If you cannot, spend some time on this to flesh out where the best transitions can be drawn from.

I find mind maps particularly helpful as a tool for speech design. When drawing your speech in a picture or image format, or as a diagram, this is a good way to tease out where the transitions can occur. As an example, let's take the idea of a speech about cats.

A speech design for a talk about cats could look like this:

Table 10 – Speech design (including Transitions) for talk about Cats

Position on mind map	Session Topic	Session detail
Centre circle	CATS	-
Top left hand corner	INTRO	Open the speech with a poem containing startling statistics about cats (that they have not heard before). ATTENTION GRABBING. Foundational Phrase = Cats are the Coolest. Then ask key Question: 'Hand straight up if you are ready to make a cat part of your life?'
<u>Transition</u>		*Use Cats are the Coolest to transition from the poem into why they are the coolest - in more detail about the origins facts and figures.*
Top of sheet- BLOCK 1	Origins	Discuss the origins of cats, history, types, context. Weave in some interactive activities. Such as each table looks into a type of cats. Works in a team. Then delivers

		back to group (could be in a role play).
<u>Transition</u>		*Use Cats are the Coolest to transition from why they are the coolest (detail) into how you can make sure you care for them in the right way.*
Right hand side- BLOCK 2	Cat care	How to take care of your cat. Practical tips. Activity - they work out a plan as to how they are going to take care of the cat from food, brushing and playing with the cat.
<u>Transition</u>		*Use Cats are the Coolest to transition from the practical tips through to the next phase of life - living with cats.*
Bottom of sheet- BLOCK 3	Life with a Cat	This session is about a feel-good session on how cats can change and improve your life for the better. Also features a series of funny cat videos - to leave them on a high.

<u>Transition</u>		*Use Cats are the Coolest to transition from the fun upbeat session we just had into the wrap up before you head home to be with your new cat.*
Summary (+ call to action)		Cats are the Coolest - summarise the three blocks, remind of the key learnings and what we achieved including a plan as to how the cat will become a part of your life. Invite final comments on what they have learnt. Call to action = buy membership to cat community and continue the sharing of info and fun pictures on cats. Then the grand finale surprise, sing them a song from Cats.

As you can see from this table, the Foundational Phrase is being used to link together the key blocks in the speech. This can work for you too, or if you have multiple Foundational Phrases they can be used as the links. List them as you go along. Both as a reminder plus as a way to show that as you move through the speech content, you are collecting them along the way and that they are key learnings for the audience to take home.

Speech ending – leave 'em on a high.

As outlined in the Table above, there is another review - this time it is of all of the points covered in the session. Then there is the most important piece of all - the Call To Action. This is where you give your audience the next step so that they can take a piece of you home with them. And then, the final gift, a surprise along with the parting message, your Foundational Phrase.

The danger of you not doing your call-to-action is huge. It is a missed opportunity. You really do need that next step. The options here are many, particularly for professional speakers:

- Back of the room sales - selling a book, CD, DVD, downloadable MP3s or other products

- Seminar - upcoming

- Coaching packages

- Other keynote speeches

- Membership sites

- These are just to name a few.

Chapter Review:

In this chapter we have examined the following topics and learnings:

I.   Explored the importance of before you start. There are two key questions to answer (or to ask then answer) before you start your speech writing. These are: (1) WHO is my audience? (2) What is their NEED?

II.   Learnt 4 steps to conduct an AUDIENCE ANALYSIS. In summary the four necessary steps are: (1) Who they are, (2) Their Traits, (3) How they think, (4) How I can help them? These questions will help you understand them and consider their perspective as you design. Remember:

      KNOWLEDGE (*yours*) + **NEEDS** (*theirs*) = **VALUE** (*you bring them*)

III. Learnt how to start your speech. The table outlines six speech openings that you can use: (1) Statistic - sharing an unusual statistic that they will not have heard previously to gain their attention, (2) Story - starting straight into a scene from the story, rather than starting by saying 'let me tell you a story about the time when..., (3) Show - a lively video with action and movement (with a purpose and link to your theme, content and message, (4) Song - something that engages yet remains relevant to the topic, (5) Share poem - a different approach, one where you could write a poem for this audience (imagine their surprise to hear a poem about them, just for them), and (6) Startling Question – attention-grabbing right away.

IV. <u>Been reminded of the importance of being bold and unique.</u> We heard the ANZAC story and how we shouldn't need to hear from others giving us permission to do something different in our speech. Don't go for plain and safe, step up and step outside the comfort zone. Make sure you get feedback first from a sample audience before trying it on your big day speech.

V. <u>Examined a sample of the keynote speech breakdown.</u> We looked into the arrangement of the body of the keynote. This can be adapted as needed to suit your style and content. Also it will depend on how much time you have as well as the audience interactive activities (where you may have 15 minutes and a report back, to use an example).

VI. <u>Toyed with Transitions and Speech Design.</u> We examined an example of a speech with the overall design of the talk, with how the transitions can be linked to the Foundational Phrase. This example on the subjects of 'Cats are the Coolest' incorporated some creative ways to start and finish the speech and interaction in between.

VII.   <u>Reviewed speech ending options</u>. Of course the way that you end is just as important as having an engaging opening to gain attention. At the end you want their attention again, so that you leave them on a high.

VIII.   <u>Examined ways to implement a call to action</u>. A most important step to take in your speaking otherwise there are missed opportunities for you to give more value to your audience and for them to fully learn from your educational materials.

What about you?

_____

_____

_____

_____

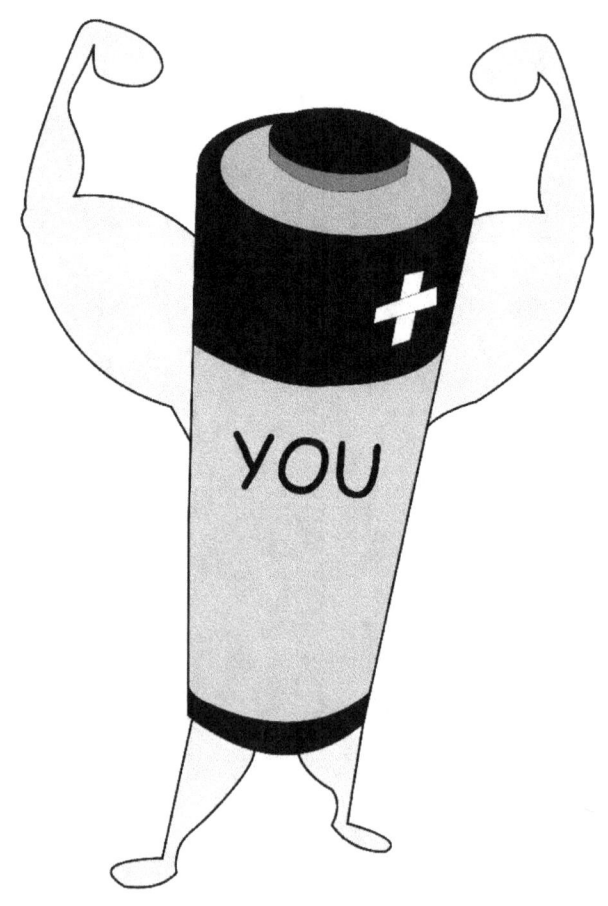

Chapter 6:

Energise

'We learn best in moments of enjoyment.'

Ralph C Smedley

Chapter 6: Energise

Whether you realise it or not, you are a ball of energy. You may however, be holding on to the wrong energy. Your audience knows this. Your audience can tell. So you had best come with the right energy to your speaking. Sometimes your energy can be modified during the speech, e.g. if you went in with high energy and you didn't match the energy of the audience. Some things in this book are optional, however this is an order.

Here are some energiser tips to get you thinking along the energiser lines:

Table 11 – Get ready to energise – 5 different methods and approaches

1	Have something fun	Have something fun for the audience to do including touch. For example, blow bubbles, balloons or a signature prop to take home. Note that the kinesthetic people will like to sit and touch it and can find this very therapeutic.	Signature Props include: Blowing bubbles Small toy Stress ball Something to hold in their hand

2	Engage at first Sight	Engage in chat. Be cheerful. When they walk into the room, call out a cheery 'good morning' (well unless it is an evening event). Smile Smile SMILE	<u>Be accessible to your audience:</u> Greet them as they come in. Be interested in them. SMILE.
3	Read your audience	As soon as they start arriving, get a feel for what your audience is feeling like. Are they chatty or are they grumpy (as in they were told they had to 'be there'). Try to make physical contact with them, shake hands as you greet them (lessens the barrier of not knowing them, moves you closer to them) and is endearing.	<u>Read 'em like a book:</u> Get a sense for the tone and mood of your people. Get a sense of who are the outgoing people. Note where they sit. Listen in to the chatter.

4	Attitude 'in check'	You need to be on your game, and above all, you need to make sure that your attitude rises above anything that could happen. If someone in your audience doesn't agree or is somewhat verbal against what you are saying or teaching, above all you need to maintain your cool.	<u>Be ready for anything:</u> It doesn't matter if your audience is not 100% with you. Be ready that they may feel differently about the subject matter.
5	Prepare You	Get yourself right and ready in order to be able to energise your audience.	<u>Preparation tips:</u> • 6-8 hours sleep (night before) • Drink water (hydrate) • No alcohol (before speaking) • Get there early - preparation • Light exercise in the morning (walk, run, sit-ups) • Say affirmations (positive) • Do something special (for the event planner)

			• Morning meditation • Eat breakfast • Minimal caffeine

Note: this is not about changing who you are or your personality (we wouldn't dream of doing that). This is about making your preparations so that they are aligned with the audience.

Energise you

'Anna, how do I do that?'

Preparation is key. Whatever is going on in your space or your private life, it doesn't come to the stage with you. It can't if you want effective energy with your audience.

So make sure you are organised. Don't leave everything to the last minute. Plan and prepare. If you have visual aids such as slides, make sure they are completed well in advance. Don't be changing them on the day of your speech. Just don't. Be more professional than that. Be drilling your speech, but not finishing it close to the day of delivery. Believe me, if you want to ace your presentation, you cannot 'wing it'.

To simplify, if you want to serve up an ace, do not wing it.

You want to 'have wings' when you speak, you don't want to 'wing it'.

Wings, not Wing.

Think about that. And lock it in.

How to prepare to be energised

How can I prepare to be organised?

As silly as that may sound, to prepare to be energised, it is so true. Your physical, mental and emotional self (or selves) can all be prepped so that they are lined up to enable your success.

Let's break this down.

Tips: Physical

- Regular exercise. Staying in shape is the ideal for leaders and speakers to perform. It is easier said than done, though get yourself into a routine that works for you to be at peak physical condition.   For you. Because when it all boils down, your health is the most important thing you have.

- Appearance. You don't have to be a guru of fashion, but you must look the part. To look 'the part' is to look the best - for you. And I believe that 10 times out of 10 that does not happen by magic. It takes effort. Gents, I am not just speaking to the ladies here either, so bring back your attention.   In fact there are increasingly higher expectations that men will look the part. 'The part' usually meaning that someone has gone to effort, to look the way they do.

- Ladies: accessories often maketh the outfit. Take efforts to match your different pieces. Psst, you don't need to spend a fortune. You can go with simple, elegant and classic - if that is who you are - and dress it up with some nice jewellery. A classic, simple look with a nice feature necklace can look fabulous. A little bit of clever effort can take you far. It is important to wear what makes you comfortable and what matches your message.

- Gents: dress a tad higher than the audience. That usually means at least a pair of black or navy trousers plus a nice shirt. If you want to suit up make sure you have a really nice tie and match your shirt, tie, cufflinks, handkerchief etc. Equally a nice shirt without tie for an entrepreneur can look good and professional. Again, your style of dress should make you comfortable and match your message.

When it comes to appearance, you don't have to figure it out alone. Grooming is of course a billion dollar industry and therefore there is help out there.

I remember seeing the fabulous documentary on the late, great Joan Rivers (RIP) where she introduces us to her personal stylist and they discuss how they work together. She (at the time) lived in New York and he lived in L.A. He comes over twice a year and puts her outfits together. That is to say, in Joan's wardrobe, there will be a dress and jacket hanging up, plus a small plastic bag containing her matching jewellery and a sticky note saying what type of event the outfit is for. Thus, she is organised and planned ahead. Her outfit is always perfectly selected well in advance to ensure that she is a complete success and matched to the audience or host. Now that's planning. I miss Joan Rivers not walking this earth.

Where you need help, ask for it, or pay a professional. If you are unsure of an event dress code, do not chance it. Ask. You don't want to run that risk.

Tips: Mental

- This is all about not letting your head chatter get in the way. Your mind is a most powerful tool. Your brain is a powerful tool. It is like your own personal CEO. It comprises 100 billion neurons (reports vary on the number there, but they all indicate that there are a lot of neurons inside).

- The thing about the brain is that it doesn't know the difference between whether you have actually done something before or not. So if you had never presented in front of 1000 people, you could 'trick' your mind into thinking you had. Then, in doing so, it would not seem like such a big deal. Does this make sense?

- *'Anna, what do you mean by 'head chatter'?'* You know the feeling. You walk into a room full of people. No one even casts a glance your way and you start to feel like: 'Should I even be here?', 'Why would anyone want to listen to what I have to say?' or 'Who do you think you are, you're no good'. Or any of innumerable variants of these types of thoughts. Your brain can be very creative when it comes to questioning your very own abilities.

- *'Anna, how can I stop this chatter?'* Take control of your mind. You should tell your brain what you want it to know. For example, if you want to deliver great value to your audience members and to serve them, to give them huge leaps and bounds forward in their personal progression, then tell your brain. Say out loud to your brain before you go to bed the night before your presentation: 'How am I going to serve my audience tomorrow to give them the best, most awesome value ever?' Then in the morning, because your brain has been searching all night and has found the answer to the question, you now know. So your statement becomes 'Today, I am going to ROCK this audience and give them the best value they could ever imagine'.

- In other words, go in with a clear mind. Go in with positive thoughts. Don't let these be derailed by anything, or anyone.

Case in point:

In the early days of my public speaking, I recall being asked to be MC at an awards luncheon. I put so much effort into the preparation that it wasn't funny. I arrived early and felt the room, practiced and made sure I knew exactly what I was in for.

On the hour, everyone started to arrive. They took their places at the tables. Seating was cabaret style. All of a sudden I spotted John, whom I knew. I bounced over to him and enthusiastically said 'Hey John.' I guess my expectation was that my greeting would be met with a similarly enthused reply. Not quite.

'Hello Anna. You're looking frightfully overdressed'.

Now, even though John made the comment with what looked like a smile on his face, I was taken aback. I quickly sized up the remark and concluded that from no point of view could that statement be taken as a compliment. Yes, John was doing his darnedest to put me off. To test my composure.

John's observation did throw me. In my mind, I started to question 'am I overdressed?' 'Perhaps I should not have worn this suit'. 'Am I going to look like a fool up there on stage?' That was 'me' then. The me that did get frazzled by such comments.

Now that I know the power of the brain, I am so much more in control of this type of scenario. Now my response would be of a very different nature (see below).

Reflecting now, over the photos taken that day, I conclude the following:

- I believe setting a standard is important - dress is part of this.

- I was not overdressed that day. I looked exactly how an MC at a formal event would be appropriately attired. I set a professional standard which set the tone for the event.

- I vowed once and for all, that I would rather be over-dressed than under-dressed. A mantra I live to this day.

(Note: I also have since learnt the value of neat casual too).

What I really learned that day was that it was John who was in the wrong. John was judging and he didn't question me in a way that served what he was trying to achieve. An example of how John could have asked the same question but in a more positive light is: 'Anna, you look professional, this must be an important event for you?' This would have held me up, and made him shine. (Remember communication 101 people. This is the art of effective influence of others. Finding out how to make it a conversation that works can be done.) Let's get along. Let's compliment each other in a genuine and well-intended manner. Let's be skilled communicators and hold each other up to shine.

The reality is that John may have had other reasons to make the comment he did. Perhaps he'd just had a fight with someone. He may not have been feeling his best. Or he could have been envious of someone or felt threatened. In any event, we can rise above pettiness, feel good and shine.

My response to the John incident would now be as follows. In my mind I would be thinking (and possibly saying to John): 'Yes John that's right. I am dressed in this way because I believe that as the MC for this event, I set the tone. I'm the leader of the event and I shall create a safe space for all of the speakers and leaders and award recipients to shine. Can you see the value in that?'

When it comes to these negative remarks and negative thoughts, give them the flick.

Ha. I just love it when you conquer something that has previously held you back.

Don't you?

Tips: Emotional

- Get into the zone. Tony Robbins calls it your 'State'. Getting into that frame where there is pure focus on the now. That peak positioning to succeed.

- If there are other things affecting you at the moment that you believe can impact the way you feel, you need to get centred. Before arriving at the venue, take a moment to pause, close your eyes and dig deep down within you. Pull up that feeling, that sentiment that is the fiercest part of you and that place from where you draw immense strength. Acknowledge this happening.

Another aspect of being prepared is your physical presence at the venue you are presenting. I'd recommend planning ahead to get there early. If you are not familiar with the room, go there prior and become one with the venue from the position of standing on the stage or speaking area.

Energising your audience

The other dynamic to this is that you want to energise your audience. So first bring your energy, then bring more energy so that they can be energised. There are two layers here.

The best way you can energise your audience, is to make the experience about them. If they can walk away feeling served by you, this is the ideal.

How can I do this?

One way to get your audience energised is to do activities that make them feel good about themselves. For example, one activity that I do with my audiences is to think for a few minutes about what their strengths are. This is when I speak on the topic of resilience.

This is a most energising activity because they focus solely on themselves for that time. Things I ask them to consider include their qualifications, attributes and skills. This is time to celebrate what is great about them as individuals or as a group.

I have found this to be a really effective activity that they enjoy. The point to the activity, and there must always be a point or learning outcome, is that they start to consider strengths that perhaps they didn't realise were so unique. I mean, have you ever had someone compliment you for something you could do and you thought 'I thought everyone could do that'.

The key here is that everyone has traits that make them unique and that not everybody has. Helping people to realise these traits can make them feel so empowered.

Another way that I bring out the fun in this topic is when I ask them to report back. I ask the audience to call out the skills, knowledge or attributes that make them great and then I acknowledge each one. This always has a fun and lively energy about it. I think this activity is a real self-esteem booster too. People love to learn something about themselves. Why not encourage them to celebrate their existing greatness?

Other energisers:

There are many activities for energising an audience. These usually involve them talking to each other, connecting and then being able to share, and include:

- Talk n' Tell. Have them team-up into little groups of 2 or more. Discuss a topic. Give them a couple of minutes. Then ask them to report back.

- Make like a... In this energising activity, you ask attendees to jump up out of their seat and behave like their favourite zoo animal for up to one minute. Another way is to ask someone what is their favourite zoo animal and then ask them all to act like that animal. Then go to the next person, and so on. When they all play along, it is a fun one. This gets them moving and refreshed.

- Sing-along. Ask the audience to sing along with a song. Put the words up on the slides or on a handout so that they know the words. Or ask them to repeat the words after you. Make sure the song is a common enough song for them to sing along to. Make it lively, fun and for there to be a point related to the learning outcome.

- Ribbon man. My favourite. Ask your audience to stand. Ask them to act like the 'ribbon man' (the figure that you see at certain service stations with air blown so they move around quickly) for thirty seconds or less. A quick and highly effective energy boost.

There are numerous examples of how you can energise your audience. The reason for doing so is always to make sure they are involved in the learning and that they are engaged and having a good time.

I recommend that if you would like to learn more about energisers and how you can play around with them, refer to training activity books.

Chapter Review:

In this chapter we have examined the following topics and learnings:

I.   Learnt that YOU are a ball of energy.

II.   <u>Explored methods for engaging your audience</u>. Via the table with 5 different methods to energise. (1) Have something fun, (2) Engage at first sight. (3) Read your audience, (4) Attitude check in, and (5) Prep You. Doing these things will bring life and energy to you, your audience and your total vibe.

III.   <u>Examined a range of tips</u>: Physical, Mental, Emotional and Other.

   A. Physical - how you present yourself.

   B. Mental - your head chatter and how your thoughts shape your behaviour. Case in point story was when I was MC at an event and was impacted by a comment made to me right before going on stage.

   C. Emotional - Get into your zone.

   D. Tips for energising your audience.

By taking charge and control of these things and planning for them, you can really enhance the experience for your audience.

What about you?

_____

_____

_____

_____

_____

_____

Chapter 7:

Entice Vocally

'We often refuse to accept an idea merely because the tone of voice in which it has been expressed is unsympathetic to us.'

Frederich Nietzsche

Chapter 7: Entice Vocally

Whose voice do you instantly recognise?

Mariah Carey, Barry White, John Lennon, Dame Edna Everidge, Ghandi, JFK, Bart Simpson, the Bee Gees, Tony Robbins, even Mr Ed the talking horse....

You have to admit, some voices you hear and you know right away who it is. Not just singing, but speaking. World leaders in many instances have a voice you would instantly recognise: Nelson Mandela, President Obama, David Cameron.

In Australia, former Prime Minister Bob Hawke had a very distinctive voice. He also had a trademark style extra (or filler) word - 'arrgh' - when he was thinking between sentences. This made him very memorable.

Dame Edna Everidge has a distinctively flamboyant voice. Remember, this is a persona created by Barrie Humphries and in doing so he has made her entirely recognisable.

What about your vocal abilities. Think about your voice. And whether anyone has given you feedback on your sound. Think about its characteristics.

Do you have a memorable voice? What feedback have you had about your voice?

_____

_____

Your voice is unique; like your fingerprints. Many people have never even considered how their speaking comes across to the listener. Whether they use a lot of extras like 'ums' and 'errs'.

I was there at the World Championship of Public Speaking when Ryan Avery was the winner. In his acceptance speech, Ryan declared that he is part of the 'like' generation. Like, you know those people who like, use the word 'like' all the time. This isn't confined only to the Gen Y-ers either. Ryan was acknowledging that there is a habit that has been formed that isn't necessarily serving those who have adopted it in everyday conversation.

He speaks fine already.

I recently phoned the office of a local politician to see how I could be of service with where he's at with his presentations. Let's call him Barry. I was fully aware that I would need to speak to Barry's executive assistant in order to secure time with him given his role and hectic schedule.

When I called Barry's office I got to speak with his executive assistant, Margaret. I ran through my normal spiel and then asked Margaret if Barry would be interested in meeting face-to-face to see if the outcomes achieved for others may be of benefit to him.

It was Margaret's reply that I found to be curious.

'No, Barry doesn't need that, he speaks fine.'

I found this reply to be interesting. I fully appreciate that Margaret's role is to ensure that Barry maximises his time and doesn't meet with absolutely everyone, and that her role is as a gatekeeper.

To suggest that a person doesn't 'need' to improve their speaking though, is a limiting belief. In my experience, we can continue to improve our speaking. If you work in an industry that involves speaking, this is even more paramount.

Context:

Over 2,000 years ago public speaking was written about in treaties and was reportedly around even before this. The Greeks invented rhetoric, the art of persuasion. As a politician, Barry's job is to persuade people to vote for him, and to give them confidence in his abilities in and even beyond his speaking.

The point of this story is that each word you speak involves your audience and how much they 'buy' your message. So every word is delivered in a tone which results in a level of genuineness or otherwise. Every word you speak can result in your audience saying Yes or No. In short, your voice is your credibility.

Your Voice is the carrier of your unique sound.

This is important.

Intonation:

Your voice delivers the message which means that in delivering that message every word counts. The way that you stress each word in a sentence can change its meaning.

Let's take the example of the following sentence and look at the different ways it could be delivered using voice:

'<u>You</u> should drive your sister there.' (emphasis on 'you' = not your father)

'You <u>should</u> drive your sister there.' (emphasis on 'should' = it's the right thing to do)

'You should <u>drive</u> your sister there.' (emphasis on 'drive' = don't walk or take the bus)

'You should drive <u>your</u> sister there.' (emphasis on 'your' = she isn't his sister)

'You should drive your <u>sister</u> there.' (emphasis on 'sister' = as opposed to your brother)

'You should drive your sister <u>there</u>.' (emphasis on 'there'=as opposed to somewhere else)

Take a few minutes to practice these sentences. Don't confine yourself to reading them out. Really give them passion and emphasis. Stand while reading them to give more energy.

Treat it like an improv activity and read in an exaggerated manner. Emphasize.

Breathing:

You must open the air flow. When you hear people who have a distinctive voice, it is usually because they are restricting the air flow in some way. For example, a person who has a breathy voice, has well and truly opened the air flow. A more common scenario is the person who has restricted the air flow.

Management of your breathing before an important speech is essential. This is in addition to your traditional style vocal warm-ups. It has been reported that ten minutes before you get up to do public speaking, your adrenaline kicks in. This causes your brain to go into 'fight or flight' mode where it decides whether there is a need for drastic action.

One key thing to do here is to ensure your breathing is controlled and regulated. This is to keep your autonomic nervous system (ANS) in order, keeping you calm and in control. A technique here is to slowly breathe in for up to ten seconds and to slowly breathe out. Both are done via the nose. Ten seconds sounds like no time at all but in fact it feels like such a long time when breathing in or out slowly. Try it now.

Organs of Articulation

Allow me to introduce you to your 'organs of articulation'. These are a cluster of organs you know well, perhaps not as a collective though.

Your organs of articulation include:

- mouth
- lips
- teeth
- tongue
- jaw
- upper and lower gums
- cheeks

When you cannot understand someone who is speaking, you might ask them to 'slow down'.

This isn't necessarily the solution though, because they are still pronouncing the words the same way - a way you find it hard to distinguish the sounds - they are just doing it slower.

This is often the response that some people whose first language is not English receive when they pronounce. They are asked to slow down their rate. When in fact, it is the rhythm patterns of the words that are being impacted and causing the words to not be recognised.

(Note: Paddy Kennedy of Kennedy Communication made this discovery over her 40 years studying this topic in relation to English as a Foreign Language.) I have enjoyed the privilege of being taught and mentored by Paddy in her accent techniques.   Check her out: www.communicatesuccess.com

Language however, is not always the barrier. What is just as important here is whether you have warmed up your organs, particularly before making an important speech.

What it means to warm up your organs of articulation is to practice pronouncing with emphasis a number of sounds, e.g. all of the vowels and consonants in the alphabet, so that your organs are ready to make any sounds by forming any words required, without the 'mumble effect' (that's a technical term.).

How do you practice? I have created a resource called the vocal warm-ups for the organs of articulation.

Here are a couple of examples of sentences for you to try (read out aloud):

1. *Can a happy dad have a bad day?* (practicing the 'A' sounds, opens the mouth)

2. *Capable like a straight whale tail.* ('A' and 'Ai' sounds, opens the mouth)

3. *We eat cream cheese. Even in the eastern sea.* ('e' and 'ea' sounds, pulls the lips back as though smiling)

4. *Kittens with mittens are forbidden to fish in Italy.* ('i' sounds)

How did you go? Did you get through them ok?

The full list of these practice sentences are available at the back of this book for you.

The benefit here is that by using greater emphasis you can get your organs more used to the practice of opening up. Especially useful on the day of any big speech, for getting your articulation primed.

Note: *the sentences themselves are silly and some make no logical sense. The purpose of them is to get your organs warmed up to make each of the sounds of the alphabet. This in turn will be a gift for your audience who will find your voice to be music to their ears.*

'Anna, how can I tell if my pronunciation or tone needs work?'

That's easy. Ask for feedback. If you'd like to send me a sample audio clip, I can advise on key words and sounds that could be improved for you. Or, you can deliver speeches and ask for feedback. It doesn't always have to come from a professional to let you in on your quirks.

Let's face it. At school we didn't have a lot of emphasis on the art of speaking. Traditionally there has been strong focus on language, i.e. English grammar, with only smatterings of debating skills and public speaking. Though even these skills don't necessarily touch on the area of how clear your diction is. There once was elocution though it doesn't seem common now.

Vocal Checklist

This is a tool that you can use to better get to know your voice. Work your way through the checklist and identify which areas you could improve on:

Table 12 – the Vocal Checklist tool

#	Vocal Aspect	Spectrum	Rating now (1 - 10)	Where you want to be?
1	Tone	Light / Serious		
2	Pitch	Low / High		
3	Pace	Slow / Fast		
4	Volume	Soft / Loud		
5	Overall sound	How is it described by others? Nasally, booming, breathy, mousy...		

Once you have completed the checklist, record your voice. Listen to your voice on the recording. See if your responses change. *Where do you hear that you could improve?*

The next step is to ensure that you ask others to give you feedback on your voice. Your voice when presenting to a group of people will no doubt sound different to when you are casually dictating it into the recording device. *What are these differences you notice?*

What have people told you about your voice? Are you a soft talker or a loud talker?

Other things you can do with your voice include experimentation. Try speaking a different way. What is the result? Does it sound better, do others treat you differently? Women tend to have higher voices, so it is good for them to practice by lowering their larynx and speaking in a lower tone.   If your voice is too high, it can (particularly in corporate environments) negatively impact your credibility. People, somewhat unfairly, may not take you as seriously. The same can often apply if you have an accent that is not clear when you speak English. You could be making the most insightful and intelligent comments, but if the sounds of the words coming out are either not clear, or the audience has to work extra hard to listen to them, it can be very challenging for you to gain the recognition and credibility you know you deserve. You need to have your ideas heard.

The best thing you can do is start to develop an ear for sound. The sounds around you. Who speaks well? Who could be a vocal role model for you to sound like? Just as we examined the idea of the confidence role model, you can also seek out a vocal role model. Perhaps Sean Connery or Oprah Winfrey.

Valuing your Voice

Your voice is unique; it is your instrument like no other. Treat your vocal instrument with care. Nurture it, experiment, take care and think of your audience and how they will receive your delivery.

If you are breathy or nasally your audience will make judgements. This is fine, as long as you acknowledge that and you don't mind. You want to be known for that because that is what makes you sound unique. That's cool.

And that is a case of being self-aware. The issue comes when you are not self-aware and people are turned off by your voice. As a speaker, you can outwardly acknowledge that your voice is like you've 'swallowed razor blades' (or insert appropriate description, preferably humorous).

If your pronunciation is lazy, your audience is forced to work too hard. Treat them better than that, unless it is part of your persona in speaking. Even then, your audience needs to understand you.

If you have become aware that you don't articulate all of your words and sounds so that they are clear, you can work on this and see results. An example of this may be the way you pronounce a sound such as words containing 'th'.

Chapter Review:

In this chapter we have examined the following topics and learnings:

I. Thought about whose voice is instantly recognisable? Considered various famous singers and world leaders whose voices we know without seeing their face.

II. Explored the origins of public speaking. We journeyed over 2000 years back in time, to ancient Greece, to discover the beginnings of rhetoric.

III. Learnt that your voice is the 'carrier of your unique sound'. We have examined the need to get to know our own voice in order to strengthen it to be the best speaker we can be. We have explored the need to get to know our own voice, to gain feedback on it, and to know its strengths and weaknesses.

IV. Learnt about our 'Organs of Articulation'. All of the organs we use to produce the sound from our mouths: lips, tongue, teeth, cheeks, gums (upper and lower), jaw etc.

V. Discovered the vocal checklist. Been introduced to this practical tool that can help you start to recognise various aspects of your voice. To understand it better, then to seek feedback and get to know how others hear you versus how you hear yourself.

The good news is that you can take control and make your own sound as clear as a bell.

What about you?

_____

_____

_____

_____

_____

_____

Chapter 8

Exhilarating Stories

'When you talk, you give yourself away. You reveal your true character in a picture which is more true and realistic than anything an artist can do for you.'

Ralph C Smedley

Chapter 8: Exhilarating Stories

As kids, Mum would read books to us like the Australian classics Blinky Bill and Cuddlepot and Snugglepie. Dad used to tell us stories about snakes growing up on the farm and scare us before bedtime. When we were old enough, I'd read The Magic Faraway Tree by Enid Blyton with characters like Jo, Bessie and Fanny. Stories take us to another place and let our imagination run wild.

We loved hearing stories as kids. *And guess what?...we still do.*

Yes, adults really enjoy hearing stories. And we learn from them. If you can tell a story in the right way so that it engages, impacts and has your audience learning, doing and feeling differently, you are set. Story has made it back into public speaking in a big way.

We engage and uplift our audience through the sensation of story. Tickle their senses. Make them picture something new.

How do we tell a great story?

Good question. I'm so glad you asked. You don't. You don't need to 'tell' the story. And you don't need to tell the audience 'now I'm going to tell you a story'. That is like telling someone about your ex on a first date. It's not the most appealing thing to draw the audience close to you. The way to do it is you allow the audience to experience your story rather than tell, or narrate it to them.

Let's take an example of the same story, told in two different ways:

Storytelling Example 1

We were driving along in Africa when our tour guide spotted some lions. We decided to get out of the car to take a closer look. They were majestic. Especially the male.

My heart pounded so hard I could feel it wanting to jump out of my chest. What was I to do next? I did what any sane person would do. I jumped back in the car screaming of course.

Storytelling Example 2

2nd December 1999. Zimbabwe, Southern Africa. Driving along open plains of the Savannah. I could feel the sun on my face. Our tour guide, Tatenda, called out from the front: 'Left hand side. 2 o'clock. Pride of Lions. Let's take a look.'

'Sure.'

'Come, let's get a bit closer.'

'Oh ok...'

Our eyes connected. He had the eyes of a King. He looked at me. All of a sudden, this King groaned and started to move. My heart skipped a beat. Although this King was used to seeing people, I instinctively realised that it was time to move away.

I looked over and Tatenda had experienced the same instincts. We were outta there.

The moral of the story: **when it comes to taking a risk, know when to walk away.**

The differences between Story 1 and Story 2:

Story 1 - is a complete narration of the details of the story scene. It describes what happened as though it is happening outside of the experience.

Story 2 - did you feel like you were there? Story 2 is like reliving the experience and having the audience experience it too. Taking them there, honing in on the details and letting them see them in their own mind, feel the way it was, heighten the senses, live and learn the lesson...and take their new-found knowledge away with them. This is the impact that a well told story can have.

The key thing that story 2 has is the foundational phrase; that core message at the end. This gives your story meaning and makes it enduring. This is the detail that will have people coming to you a day, week, month and even years later to say 'I still remember that story you told us about being in Africa and the lions'.

The great thing about writing good stories is that all you need to do is have some techniques, and the rest.... well, you have the material within you.

Here are some essential ingredients that, when cooking up your next story, you need to include:

Table 13 – Six Ps – the Essential Elements of Successful Storytelling

#	Key ingredient	Detail	How to use
1	**People**	Who are the people who feature in your story? There might be other characters aside from people, such as animals or other subjects.	People make the story come to life. Decide the following: • Identify who is in your story. • What is their unique identity? • How do they express themselves?

			<ul><li>What are their quirks?</li><li>How do they relate to others?</li><li>Are they necessary in the story?</li></ul>
2	**Parlance**	Parlance is a French word for speaking. This is about what the People in your story say, and the way or manner that they speak. The way that they do must add to the telling of your story. Make sure that you use Parlance. This is all about the People in the story having lines that they say. Parlance is here to prevent you from having too much narrative. Move away from 'describing' what happened, to having it come to life through Parlance.	This relates to how the People (and other characters or things) in your story speak:<ul><li>What do they say?</li><li>How do they say it?</li><li>How can you make them uniquely stand out in the story?</li></ul>

3	**Punchlines**	Punchlines are Parlance with panache that pack a punch.	Punchlines don't have to be hilarious comedic lines. They can be subtle, fresh and sublime.
		These are humour lines in your story.	Use the punchline to reveal a lively or interesting comment.
		The colourful parts that bring out the punchline which can be funny or revealing or surprising. Don't be afraid to deliver your lines with emphasis and confidence.	If it is not as funny as you think it could be, try to rearrange the words or the sequence of the sentences to see if they can work another way.
			If you don't think your line is funny enough, practice practice practice in different ways to give it more animation. Find the way that works best for that line.

| 4 | **Pithy** | Don't waffle in your story, please. You will lose your audience if it takes too long to get to the point of the story. Your stories should be succinct, pointed and concise.

Your audience starts tuning out if you don't give them some lift or point within a brief amount of time. That amount of time is seconds. You have only a matter of seconds before your audience is tuning out and looking at their smartphone. | Here are some ways to ensure you get to the point with your story:

When you practice your story, record it (via audio and video) and review. Where can you cut it down?

Have your stories written down or typed out. Read through the story and work out where you can cut out sentences and words that are not adding real value to the story. Find those nuggets that are the key things the audience must know. Not the fluffy sidelines decorating the story. |

| 5 | **Purpose** | This is about getting to the point of your story. The purpose is the key walkaway you want your audience to learn, to remember and to live.

For example, my Foundational Phrase for the topic of resilience is '*Find something SWEET in every defeat*'. Here I can have an image on my slides to match this, or I can hand out a sweet for the audience to remember me by.

When I delivered such a speech in Perth at a conference, the next day I was walking past a cafe and someone yelled out 'Hey, there's Mrs Sweet.' | EVERY story has a meaning and Purpose. It is the reason for delivering it. Your Foundational Phrase should be:

• Short, sweet and catchy.

• Memorable - in years to come.

• Vivid - able to see an image with it. |
| 6 | **Pause** | Please please please, oh please, use..... Pause. The pause is your best friend when it comes to enhancing delivery of your story, and your secret weapon in adding anticipation and suspense. | Always have pauses in your presentations. |

Two types of Pauses

Pauses are not optional. Pauses are a fundamental part of speaking, whether in conversation, or with your audience. Pauses are even more special when it comes to storytelling. Two types of pause that you can use are:

- Natural Pause - always use this pause as part of your speaking. Pauses should be placed naturally between, and during, sentences when public speaking. When you see a full stop, comma, semi-colon etc, there is a pause naturally following this. The reason we know this is because we know that when we converse, we have to take a breath. Our sentences do not run into each other; nor do they run breathlessly from start to finish. We have punctuation to remind us of this in the written word, and we have the pause to remind us of this in the spoken word.

- Dramatic Pause - use this tool for impact in your story. When you want to have the audience hanging on your words, or when introducing anticipation, the dramatic pause is perfect. Dramatic pauses can be longer than natural pauses. They can be partnered up with body language to add extra drama or increase comic effect. Facial gestures, expressions and body actions and poses can also greatly enhance this storytelling tool.

And one to avoid:

- *Pregnant Pause* – *the curse of the under-prepared public speaker. But don't worry, it primarily affects only those unwary speakers who haven't learned and practiced the lessons and exercises laid out in this volume.* ☺

Pauses are the most powerful of tools and yet the ones that often get left behind. It takes real confidence to deliver a story with pause.

How confident are you to present with Pause?

Bringing out humour in stories

Stepping out onto the street, I could tell I was in Los Angeles, California. I could feel the hot sun on my skin, I could smell the suntan lotion and I could hear the traffic on the seven lane highway. I had arrived. L.A. here I am.

My driver, Bill, was a chatty fellow. Bill didn't take a breath the whole trip from LAX to Northridge (45 mins):

'You heard of Tom Selleck?'

'Sure - three men and a baby - hilarious.'

'Yeah and Magnum PI. I went to school with him. He's done well for himself, real well. And he's a good guy too.'

Bill sure knew how to name drop. I didn't mind one bit, it was all interesting to me. Made me feel closer to fame (*hey a girl can dream can't she?.....*).

Through all the name dropping, there was one comment that stuck out though.

'I'm 71 years old.'

'Wow, you sure don't look it. What's your secret?'

'My secret you ask?... Well, I don't drink or smoke......... haven't done so for near on forty years now........ oh yeah, but come to think of it, I sure could use a cold one right now!'

The great thing about Bill is he is a character. You don't have to make up information about Bill. He just is. Full of character. You don't need a scriptwriter for someone like Bill. The lines that came from him were classic. Without him even trying, or without me prying, ha.

Life is full of Bills. People you meet who are interesting, lively and bring something colourful to the everyday. Taking note of these people (and taking notes.) can lead to some great stories for your presentations.

I think that this is fantastic news for all of us who are not comedians. My brother Simon was always the joker of our family. He was always saying something silly that would have us all chuckling. Whereas my attempts at humour would usually be met with puzzled blank looks. Even when I added a smile or laugh at the end (symbolising my attempt at humour), I still didn't reach the heights of receiving loads of laughter out loud.

The good news here is that even the unfunny among us can extend into the humour stakes. I learnt this from humourist Jeanne Robertson CSP CPAE. When I realised this lesson, I felt like I had gained entry into one of those cool nightclubs where everyone lines up outside for hours on end, by jumping the queue, and gotten in for free.

Humour can come out naturally. It is all around us. Start looking for it in your life.

Where can you think of instances of humour right now?

_____

_____

_____

_____

_____

While I was in Los Angeles, during the writing of this book, I stayed with Colleen and Frank. The loveliest people you could ever imagine. The most wonderful bed n' breakfast hosts. EVER. The day would start out with freshly brewed coffee, served up in the giant white coffee cup that was ready for me each morning. I was allowed to sit out in the back yard with the most beautiful, inviting pool that you can imagine.

One morning, while writing and sitting out in the backyard, Colleen came out the back door:

'I'm thinking of contacting Apple to see if they can use you'.

'Oh?..... What for?'

'In an advertisement. Your purple top, your necklace, earrings, bright pink fingernails all matches your computer. We may as well take a picture; it's like you're already doing an ad for them.'

If you ever want to visit Colleen and Frank's piece of paradise, let me know. They are the most welcoming of hosts. You've heard of the Holiday Inn, I call their place the 'Paradise Inn'.

Throughout the course of my stay, Frank made several references to my book writing. It got to the extent that he decided he wanted to write a book too. I agreed that it was a great idea that he should write a book. A couple of days later the idea popped into my head that, together, they could write a coffee table type book, with pictures of all of their different bed and breakfast guests. Frank didn't hesitate to come out with a corker:

'Oh yeah, and you should see what there's going to be about YOU in there.'

I burst out laughing. 'Um yeah, maybe that's not such a good idea after all.'

Chapter Review:

In this chapter we have examined the following topics and learnings:

I.   <u>Explored how stories are a part of life</u>. Not just for children, adults equally engage with story and can learn from them. So include story to engage your people, no matter how corporate they are.

II.   <u>Examined two versions of a story</u>. The African Lion story. Version 1 was a narration of the story told from outside the story. Version 2 was a more engaging version of the story including dialogue, characters, movement and action. Most of all, version 2 had a message and Foundational Phrase the audience could walk away with.

III. <u>Six Ps - the Essential Elements to Successful Storytelling</u>. Bringing out the key ingredients such as People, Parlance, Punchlines, make it Pithy, have Purpose and recognise the power of Pause.

IV.   <u>Importance of Pause</u>. We have examined ....Pause as a mandatory tool in speaking. We learnt about the two types of pauses being Natural pause and Dramatic pause. We addressed ways that you can practice having pauses in your speaking and how you can teach yourself to do so.

V.   <u>Identified bringing out humour</u>. Even if you don't consider yourself a 'funny' person, the news is all good.....because humour occurs all around us. Just listen to the classic lines you hear in your everyday life. Start to tune in your humour ear, write down those classic moments and watch them appear in your material. I can hear the laughter from here.

What about you?

_____

_____

_____

_____

_____

Chapter 9

Express Visually

'Educating the mind
without educating the
heart is no education.'

Aristotle

Chapter 9: Express Visually

Imagine a beautiful painting. Think about the colour and texture of that painting. Is it made up of water colours or bright colours? It may be a painting done by your son or daughter at school. And it hangs proudly on the fridge door. Or it may be a masterpiece from the Renaissance hanging in a museum.

Let's look at the example of the famous painting: ***Luncheon of the Boating Party*** (1880-1881). In French it is called *Le déjeuner des canotiers*. The painting is by French impressionist Pierre-Auguste Renoir.

This celebrated painting is a lively snapshot in time of a group of people enjoying themselves at a riverside restaurant. There are approximately 14 characters in the painting ranging from people who are dressed up, e.g. in a top hat in the case of the wealthy art historian to more casually dressed characters such as those wearing a singlet. There are also people in the midst of various activities such as drinking, leaning on the balcony and even (according to descriptions) flirting. There is a lady drinking from a glass, while another plays with or talks to her dog at the table which is filled with glasses, wine and food.

The painting is a lively recollection of an event that really leaps out of the frame at you. You can get a real sense of the occasion. So engaging is this picture that I understand it was the subject of a novel by another author in more recent times.

Do Renoir and his beautiful painting have relevance to public speaking?

I believe yes.

Visuals. Renoir's painting demonstrates how visuals can take you to another place. The 'look and feel' of something can mean the difference between good and great. So, too, can your presentation have a look and feel for your audience to experience.

This is not limited to you and how you personally present, although this is crucial. It also extends to the visual aids that you select to help with your presentation.

Case in point:

Sally and Sarah are both speakers at the same industry event. There are a couple of months until the event and plenty of time to prepare. Both Sally and Sarah are working on their presentations to make sure that they are top notch. This is a significant event for them both as it can mean the difference between gaining new clients and keeping the current accounts that are very important to their firm.

Speaker 1 – Sally

Sally decides she will use PowerPoint slides. She has 45 minutes to speak, and she doesn't want to miss out of any key points. Sally puts together 40 slides with all of the data and information she knows the audience will appreciate. They won't be walking out wondering about this topic. Sally is so busy that she doesn't have time to prepare a handout. The information in the slide show and what Sally plans to say in the allotted time will be sufficient, Sally believes.

Speaker 2 – Sarah

Sarah needs to better understand her audience. So she contacts the event organiser. She asks about the priorities of the audience. Sarah also asks if she can gain some input from members of the audience beforehand. The event organiser allows her to send through a quick survey which she uses to engage a few of the audience members and understand their needs beforehand. This information is invaluable. Sarah better understands what they know, what they need to know more about, and what they want to know how to do most.

Sarah is also going to use slides, though she uses a Mac so it will be a presentation slide show in Keynote (the Mac equivalent of PowerPoint). Sarah has the same 45 minutes to cover her topic. Somewhat different to Sally, Sarah prepares only 15 slides to cover the topic. Sarah is going to use images that fill the screen to make the slides jump out and really engage the audience. Sarah will also use creative techniques to have the slides come to life. Such as a couple of animation techniques to illustrate a key learning point, not simply for novelty's sake.

Of the two presentations, which one is going to be more successful at connecting with the audience?

Sarah's. She has considered her audience, keeping them in mind while designing her speech. Thus, Sarah does the following key things:

- Conducts an audience analysis to understand this particular audience's needs.

- Was in contact with the event planner beforehand and even got a sample of people to complete a survey in advance.

- Designs the slides noting that she has 45 minutes in her session and that she doesn't want to rush, determines a suitable pace.

- Considers the way that the whole package looks and feels from an audience perspective. This includes the branding and how the colour scheme of the slides and the handout all need to link back to Sarah and her content.

- Seeks help with putting it all together - Sarah understands the value of this and she wants to leave a lasting impact.

- Considers all learning types - from the data-focused people to the visual learners.

- Thinks about how she can leave an enduring impact - gives to her audience, including the handout and the Call to Action.

- Call to Action - gives her audience another way to improve in this area of expertise - come along to learn more at my 1 day workshop.

- Arrives early, circulates with the audience members, says 'Hi' and shakes their hand, SMILES.

What are the things that Sally does that do not work?

- Goes straight into the content before understanding the audience. Talks about what she knows and 'thinks' the audience needs to know without any verification on whether this is relevant to their current needs.

- Doesn't consider the allotted time and how to manage it effectively in terms of how much content can be included.

- Too much data and information overload.

- Too many slides in the allotted time.

- Not thinking about the visual impact of the slides and the overall package.

- Assuming she will be fine putting it all together and 'hoping' it will be fine on the day.

- Not having a Call to Action.

The approach taken by Sally (Speaker 1) is an all too common occurrence. This is exactly how someone who is not practiced at the skills of speaking will approach their speech. It is not surprising either. When you have not been coached or had the right teachings it is only natural to do so.

There are good lessons in this scenario. Even well intended people can think they are offering value to their audience, but when it boils down to it, they end up doing a disservice to them. Not winging your presentation is key here. If you are not doing this all the time, you are likely going to need some outside help. If you are doing this regularly i.e. speaking to audiences, you are still going to need to maintain a level of freshness by seeking new ideas and feedback on what you are doing. You always need to keep a step ahead of the game.

There are many ways you can express yourself visually in your presentations.

Table 14 – 7 Methods to express visually in your presentations

#	Method	Detail	How
1	**Slides**	Either PowerPoint (windows) or Keynote (Mac).	Use your slides as a visual enhancement, NOT the sole focus for people to look at. Slides are not the main show, they are a support act to enhance, add interest and variety. Make sure your slides have diversity. There should be a lot of imagery, rather than words. No over-crowding of slides allowed though, including too much information. Don't overload with data.
2	**Prop**	Use a signature (branded) prop that your audience can take home with them. Examples include: pen, blowing bubbles, magnets, USB stick, toy.	Find a prop that matches your message. Provide as a keepsake to help lock in your core teachings and message. Fun props are best.

| 3 | **Video** | You can use video and have it playing as your audience enters the room - a visual stimulant. You could create a video which actually incorporates your audience. | Mingle before your keynote. If it's a conference, get some photos of people socialising, networking; take these and use them as your opening slideshow. They will see themselves as part of the show before you even begin, and they will feel like....WOW. |
| 4 | **Photos** | Use uplifting, inspirational, aspirational photos to make your audience feel good and like they want to strive for more. Important: Have your images large enough to fill up the entire slide - limit to a few words per slide if needed. Make your PowerPoint slides impactful and uplifting. | Obtain or purchase top quality images for your presentations. You can use your own too if they are quality images. Use to motivate and uplift your audience. |

5	Audience - one Audience - many	You can use your audience members to enhance the light, colour and movement of your presentation. Rather than it just being you up there, by bringing up someone from the audience, it is more vibrant and stimulating.	For example, you could have people come to the front as in presenting results to a question you posed where you are reporting back. Also, you can have a volunteer from the audience who wants to 'role play' their particular piece - whether a speech or story - and you give feedback and workshop on the spot with audience interaction.
6	Handouts	Handouts can be used to cement in your learnings. Your handouts should be: - Succinct. - Interactive (i.e. space for them to write down their reflections. - Appropriately branded.	Plan your handouts. Don't make them overly complicated. A one page, double sided handout can be effective. Don't waste paper. A small sized booklet works too. Consider the handout for maximum interaction - design it around your audience member. What would they want to see? Ask them.

		- Including your contact details and a call to action.	
7	**You**	Your presentation of yourself. * Make sure that you present yourself well. Ideally your presentation of you should match in with your branding look and tone. Your brand is of course, the tone you want to set. Doing this brings a continuity and a consistency to you. In essence, if there is a common thread running through all that you do, this in turn sends a message to your audience that you are consistent with this message. This also shines through for your values such as reliability. If you are seen as reliable by your audience, they	Reference: 4 Ps to Confidence Creation.

		are more likely to trust and believe in your teachings.	

There is much more to YOU than your presentation of you. There is a whole complete (pardon the pun) body of work on body and stagecraft.

Body and Stagecraft

Whether you realise it or not, every move you make on stage gets noticed. It's a little bit like a first date in that way... your every move is being critiqued and if you make one move out of place....BAM. You are considered not suitable and you are back to being single. Back to square one.

You don't want to have to go back to square one in your speaking. Let's take a look at some of the nervous habits I have seen people display when they first start to speak in front of an audience:

• <u>Awkwardness</u> - this is represented by strange posturing. Common examples include leaning on one leg, crossing one leg over the other, switching from one leg to the other, general fidgeting (such as the jingle jangle of change in pockets), and rocking back and forth.

- Body covering - using the arms to shield the front of the body. This could be folding the arms (either half or in full), crunching in the elbows so that it looks like they are clutching on for dear life or stitched to the side of the body, clasping hands in front, or playing with an object (such as a pen). All of these poses either create a barrier between the speaker and audience member, or in the case of the pen, cause the audience member to be distracted or focused on the offending object. Thereby losing the attention of the audience.

- Averted eye gaze - where the speaker is not in control of their eye contact. He or she is not confidently and purposefully making the eye contact with the members of the audience in a meaningful and connecting way.

- Fly-away arms - this is when the arms start flying around some may say over-enthusiastically, though in particular, they are uncontrolled. Arms and hands, when moved in a certain way, can be highly effective. The key one to watch from my observations is the continuous parallel gestures. That is when the hands / arms are moving in exactly the same way over and over. An example: *'Hi, my name is (circle gesture arms) Anna. I am a (circle gesture arms) speaking stylist.'* It makes the audience feel as though the same thing is being said which causes them to switch off (note: often when this is happening, the rhythm of the voice is also working in a repetitive way). Be mindful of this one.

- <u>Verbal security blankets</u> - these are all of the filler or extra words that we hear when we should hear a pause sound. Such as um, err, like, you know, actually, approximately.... you get the picture.

<u>Note</u>: these mistakes are all completely natural. That is why most human beings adopt them.

'Ok Anna, we get it.....but how can we lose these gestures once and for all?'

It is a natural defence mechanism by our body to adopt these positions. What we need to tell ourselves, and reprogram the mind to think is that it is ok for our hands to be freed from covering the body. It is perfectly ok. Nothing bad will happen if we expose our middle body area by not covering it with our arms. Also that the consequences of us not having to cover our body will result in a much greater audience response. From a rational viewpoint, our audience will be brought closer to us. They are much more likely to find you an inspiration if your body is open to them, rather than closed off.

This is the great news - you CAN change your habits.

Now that we have examined these, here are some body principles to live by. By following these golden rules in terms of your positioning, you will by default not make the mistakes outlined above.

Table 15 - 5 Techniques for strong body positioning and gestures

#	Technique	Application
1	**Stance / Posture**	- First and foremost start grounded, i.e. feet firmly planted on the ground demonstrating confidence. Also command the stage you stand upon. - If you have an issue in this area where you cannot control your body, practice standing in front of the mirror and speaking while not moving your body. If this poses a challenge, get a book and stand reading it aloud while holding it in one hand and standing firmly without moving or shifting. Focus on planting your feet firmly on the ground. - Try some visualisation activities where you picture yourself standing in front of an audience of people while speaking. Picture yourself with feet firmly grounded. Picture this regularly, i.e. daily for a couple of weeks. Then try it for real.

2	Hands / Arms	- I recommend that if this area is an issue for you, start with a neutral body position and use one hand only for effect. This will eliminate the parallel gesture issue and the fly-away arms.
		- In using hands and arms in front of body, use the open palms to show that you come in peaceful manner and are not hiding anything through your body.
		- Use fingers - to exaggerate numbers or points that you want to make. Hold your hands up high when doing so to illustrate command of body use.
		- Don't be afraid to have wide, high and low arm gestures. We don't often see someone using their arms so greatly unless they are super confident. Now, you can too.
3	Eyes	- Seek to meet the eyes of each and every person in your audience. Hold the gaze for a couple of seconds before moving to another point in the audience. This should be greatly varied in your approach. For example, if you look to the left front person, next switch your gaze to look to someone at the right back. This variety will ensure you do not lose people in the audience because they feel ignored that you haven't 'looked their way'. Also, it gives some feeling of not being predictable. You also want to be

		able to see what all people in the audience are doing, and that you haven't lost them.
		- Where you have an extremely large audience, i.e. thousands, identify checkpoints at each corner of the audience (and centrally within those seated areas) and ensure that you look in the direction maintaining the gaze for some time.
4	**Words (verbal instincts)**	There are a number of ways that you can prepare yourself for fewer words you don't mean to say (such as um).
		Here are some ways:
		- Practice reading aloud. At the end of each sentence, pause before starting the next sentence. Read the words with emphasis as though making it sound very interesting.
		- Practice talking about a subject where you don't have a script and you are speaking off the cuff or without preparation (impromptu).
		- Record your voice speaking (audio) in an impromptu manner, or practicing a story or part of your speech. Use this process of recording and listening over, as a way to hear how many of these words are appearing, and to iron out the verbal creases so to speak.

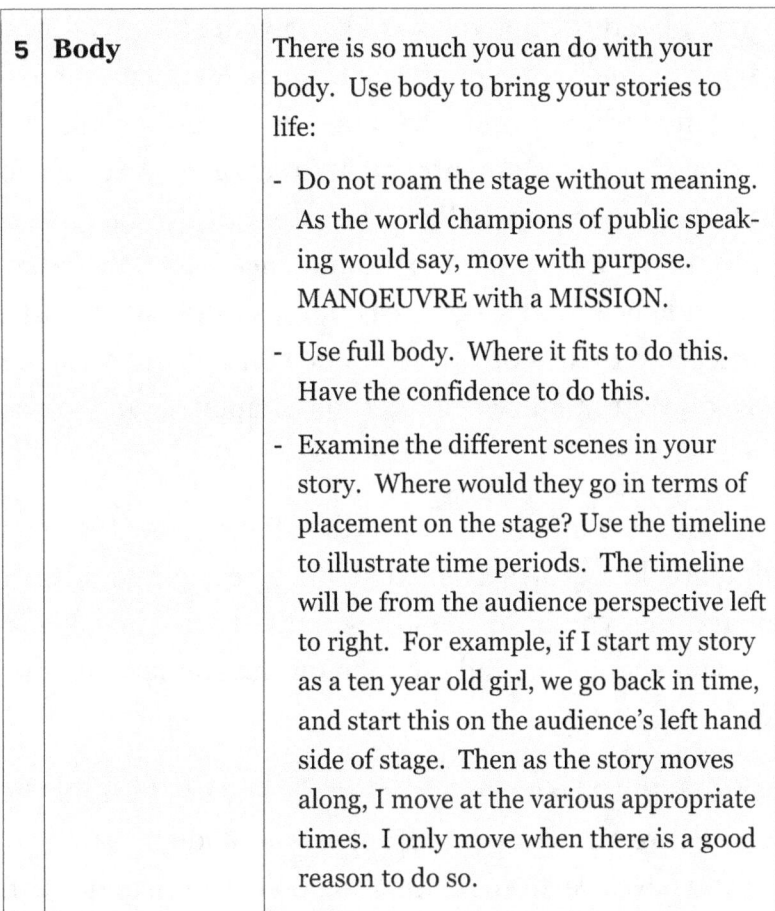

5	Body	There is so much you can do with your body. Use body to bring your stories to life:
		- Do not roam the stage without meaning. As the world champions of public speaking would say, move with purpose. MANOEUVRE with a MISSION.
		- Use full body. Where it fits to do this. Have the confidence to do this.
		- Examine the different scenes in your story. Where would they go in terms of placement on the stage? Use the timeline to illustrate time periods. The timeline will be from the audience perspective left to right. For example, if I start my story as a ten year old girl, we go back in time, and start this on the audience's left hand side of stage. Then as the story moves along, I move at the various appropriate times. I only move when there is a good reason to do so.

Stagecraft and Placement

The front and centre of the stage, centre stage is the power position. This is where you would, in most cases, start your speech and then move around the stage from there. Depending of course where your stories take you and where the various scenes in your stories are.

We have already explored how to bring your stories out in an engaging manner. Stagecraft can bring them out even more. Stagecraft is where you use the stage as a prop, a giant prop that forms the environment for you to shine in. An arena for you to bring your story to life. The extent to how far you can go with this is basically tied to the audience. Not only the size of the audience (and stage area) but also the nature of the audience and their NEEDS. (How do you find out about the needs of your audience? Refer to Chapter 1 and do an audience analysis).

First, it takes confidence to use the stage. Now that your confidence has grown from making sure your mindset is right and that you have all of the required speaking skills at hand, you should be ready to take on the confidence of the stage.

What does this mean, confidence of the stage? It means that when you are on the stage in front of your audience, that you do as you have practiced to do. You don't all of a sudden turn into a shy little mouse who thinks 'I don't need to do it the way I practiced, all will be fine, the audience will get it.' No no no. It means that you stand your ground. You drill that speech beforehand and then you get up and deliver it. You deliver it to your audience so well that they think you are the most compelling and captivating speaker they have seen, PLUS they learn from you.

It means that if you are sharing a story such as the Africa Lion taking risks story, that you show the different scenes. First the one where you paint the scene of Zimbabwe. Then you show the vehicle scene with tour guide, Tatenda.

How to use a Timeline

When you use the stage, we have established that you only move when there is reason to do so. You move with purpose, or MANOEUVRE with a MISSION. The timeline method can help you do this. The timeline moves from the audience's left to right. In other words left to right from what the audience can see. (Note: this will be you, as the speaker, moving right to left as you are facing the other way). Here is an example of how a timeline can work using the Africa Lion story:

Scene 1 - Start at centre stage. Position firm and grounded. Set the scene: '2nd December 1999. Zimbabwe, Southern Africa.'

Scene 2 - Move from centre stage to the audience's far left (back a bit). Narration mode: *Driving along open plains of the Savannah. I could feel the sun on my face. Our tour guide, Tatenda, called out from the front: 'Left hand side. 2 o'clock. Pride of Lions. Let's take a look.'* [Move across the timeline a little to demonstrate movement as the action happens.]

Tatenda slowly manoeuvred the vehicle closer. Little by little. (Note: Tatenda's voice can be delivered with a Zimbabwean accent.)

Scene 3 - [Stop moving on stage.] *Tatenda stopped the vehicle.* [Stay stationary and gesture / body movement as though seeing the lion just over there. Use body to build the anticipation.] '*C'mon, let's get a little bit closer.*' [Show the action that Tatenda is getting out of the vehicle.] '*Oh ok...*' [Say this showing you were hesitant.]

Scene 4 - [Move a little more across the stage / timeline.] 'He had the eyes of a King. The King of the jungle. I looked at him. He looked at me. All of a sudden, as I was admiring his Majesty, this King groaned and started to move. My heart skipped a beat. Although this King was used to seeing people, I instinctively realised that it was time to move away.' [Show moving back to car.] 'I looked over and Tatenda had experienced the same instincts. We were outta there.' [Show the actions and look relieved as you swiftly drive away.]

Scene 5 - Move back to centre stage to be grounded and to deliver the learning:

'The moral of the story:

When it comes to taking a risk, know when to walk (or in some cases run) away.'

This is an example of how you can use a timeline. You can get creative with it. The most important thing to do however, is to make sure that the audience understands why you are moving, where everything is placed on the stage and that they can relate to it. You don't want to have the effect of having them losing your track of thought or not understanding why you were moving around. You don't want them to think they are on a ride at Disneyland either. Make it clean, crisp, clear and easy to follow and you'll set-up a great visual experience for your audience.

Being a great speaker doesn't come by accident. It takes time, crafting, re-crafting and feedback to create that masterpiece of yours.

Chapter Review:

In this chapter we have examined the following topics and learnings:

I. <u>Explored the importance of visual in your presentation</u>. Using Renoir's Luncheon of the Boating Party classic painting, we reminded ourselves of, and delved into some detail around, what makes a visual compelling and how this relates to public speaking and you in the way you present.

II. <u>Learnt through the example of Sally and Sarah</u>. Exactly what can happen when you are invited to present. If you are not on top of your planning and preparation, your speech can end up being mediocre - every speaker's greatest fear. If you are on top of it, in the case of Sarah, the experience of your audience is so much greater, more valuable, it can change lives and leave the impact you should want to leave. We did a breakdown of why each approach either worked or didn't have the impact desired.

III. <u>Seen the 7 methods to express visually</u>. Using (1) Slides (to enhance message not to be the message), (2) Props - especially a prop they can take home to remember your learning by, (3) Video - to engage, create emotional connections, stir excitement and add to what you bring (again shouldn't be the sole focus),

(4) Audience - one member from the audience to workshop, (5) Audience - using multiple people from the audience to work through an issue, (6) Photos - great to create fun and energy, make your images take up the whole slide and minimise words if they are needed at all - go for impactful and uplifting visuals in your slides (images not words), and (7) You. The energy you bring is your most important visual. Make sure it's fantastic, both in appearance and in body language / movement.

IV.   <u>Viewed body and stagecraft mistakes people make</u>. These covered (1) Awkwardness in movement, (2) Body covering such as arms, (3) Averted eye gaze - instead of eye contact that connects, (4) Fly-away arms that are out of control, and (5) Verbal security blankets including errs, ums and you knows.

V.   <u>Resolved these through the 5 techniques for strong body positioning and gestures.</u>   (1) Stance and posturing, (2) Hands, (3) Eyes and (4) Words and (5) Body. Looked into methods and techniques to adopt to avoid the mistakes and to embrace the confident presenter you know you are.

VI.   <u>Looked into stagecraft and placement</u>. We examined the centre stage position, the neutral stance for positioning. In particular, how you can start your presentation grounded in the power position and then move out from there, particularly when branching into a story or an activity. Also, stressed the importance to MANOEUVRE with a MISSION. When you move on stage it is never because you are wandering aimlessly or through nerves.

VII.   <u>Encountered the timeline</u>. This approach to storytelling in particular is key to keeping your audience's attention and making your story crystal clear. Starting on the audience's left hand side is the earlier point in time, to move through time you can move across to the audience's right hand side of the stage to illustrate travelling through time. Note, this is not needed for all stories but it is highly impactful when used correctly.

What about you?

_____

_____

_____

_____

_____

_____

Chapter 10

Enhanced Preparation

'Comfortable is ok,
but don't you want to
shine like a diamond?'

Jana Barnhill

Chapter 10: Enhanced Preparation

How can I bring my 'A' game every time I speak to my audience?

Preparation. What this means is get on the front foot, be ahead of the curve and ride the wave when it is high. Sounds like fun doesn't it?

It may also sound like it requires time. Yes, as things in which you want to reach mastery invariably do. Time may be something you don't have a lot of. If this is the case, do what you can do for you. If speaking is not your main thing and you are a leader of people in a flat out job that demands of you constantly, then I suggest booking in time for speaking. Book in time to craft, prepare, practice, drill and gain feedback via coaching (<u>note</u>: *having a good coach helps*).

This chapter therefore explores methods you can use to be best prepared. Some believe they can wing-it, but they cannot. The reason is because audiences expect more from you. They want to be inspired, energised, moved. You don't achieve that without planning.

Let's take a closer look at this scenario:

Wings, not Wing

Two months ago Wendy asked you to deliver a presentation to the Board at the upcoming Annual General Meeting. Of course at the time, you gladly agreed. It seemed like a fine idea back then, and there was plenty of time to prepare... Now, with just days before the meeting, the presentation is looming, with the date creeping inexorably up on you. You haven't had a chance to get to it though. After all, you're a busy executive with a ton of items on your to-do list.

Sound familiar? What is there left to do?... Oh well, I'll just 'wing-it'.

Ba-Bow. Fail. Major recalculation needed.

Sadly, this is an all too common occurrence. It could also be described as, well, the public speaking elephant in the room. Only this elephant isn't ready to speak, because he hasn't had time to prepare. He is trying to hide in the corner of the room but he stands out quite a bit.

Folks, this is the public speaking version of committing a sin. Winging your presentation is not a plan, nor is it professional. You may be thinking one of these thoughts right now:

- *'They'll never know.'* (Reality check = they know.)

- *'I perform better under pressure.'* (Reality check = you perform better when you have considered how you can deliver value to your audience.)

- *'I just haven't had the time.'* (Reality check = you haven't <u>made</u> the time for this to be a priority - if you aren't prepared, you shouldn't speak.)

- *'I'm a busy executive.'* (Yes, so are thousands of others. They can do it.)

- *'They've heard all this before.'* (Reality check = really? if that's the case, you need to freshen up your act, sunshine.)

If any of these sentiments resonate with you, tut-tut. Note the reality check comments. These comments represent the lazy person's public speaking. Now this has been brought to your attention, make sure you don't commit one of these.

Techniques

Do techniques around planning for speaking exist?

Sure they do *(and the crowd goes wild)*. These techniques and tips are not speaking tips, more around the organisation (and rehearsal) of speaking and presenting.

Here they are:

1. <u>Book in time to prepare</u> - put multiple appointments in the calendar (speechwriting time, coaching, drills, rehearsals, before the day, on the day preparations, post presentation actions). Treat it like any other big commitment - the more you plan the smoother the end result will run.

2. <u>For major keynote presentations</u> - have the presentation ready months in advance, ideally locking in the content no less than one month prior to the presentation. If you don't have months to prepare, try to have it written upfront, lock it in and then drill until the day.

3. <u>Plan your impromptu speeches</u>. If you know of a particular question you will be asked, work on a short piece forming your response in a way that makes it interesting for your audience. For example, when I speak about my combined Australian and French ancestry, I jokingly claim that for breakfast I eat toast with butter, vegemite and snails! I have worked this short, light-hearted introduction, tried it on people and then re-crafted it to make it as succinct as it possibly can be. Works a treat (on Aussie audiences that is).

4. <u>Drill, drill, drill</u> - you can guess what's coming here. Drill your speech daily. Run through it, even if you don't feel like it. Don't let your mind tell you that you don't 'need' to or that you don't 'feel' like doing it. Just

crack on and drill that baby till it is leaping out of your body. Example of why: *when I first learnt to pitch my business, I learnt the words and then I drilled them. The first time I recorded it, it sounded terrible. It was lacking emphasis and sounded raw. Drill drill drill drill. I recorded it again. I kept the original recording and put next to the drilled version, they are like chalk and cheese.* You can tell the version that fits like a glove versus the awkward 'learning how to walk' version.

5. <u>Plan your interaction.</u> Of course, you want to have interaction and audience engagement. This should not however, be entirely spontaneous. You need to have an idea about when and linked to what learning outcomes or pieces. For example, I recommend that you have an interaction with your audience within the first minute of your presentation. That could be as simple as asking a question of your audience: 'raise your hand if the thought of public speaking makes you nervous? Ok, that's approximately 90% of the room. The reason I ask is because research says it is 75% of people experience glossophobia'...etc. This is a simple and effective method. Or, you could start with using a tool like 'animoto' where you take photos beforehand and then it creates a video that you have playing while they are coming into the room. Or, you can use social media before the event to engage. Many ways are

available, make sure you consider which suits your style and what you are comfortable in doing.

6. <u>Improve elocution</u>. This one is for those speakers who are super keen to improve and want to get to the next level, fast. I mean those who are serious about this. If you want to be up there with the best, every single word, every sound and movement when you are on stage, counts. Practicing the foundations such as elocution and improving your clarity of diction is a must. Contact me for ways to practice. By improving how you sound, your audience can listen effortlessly to you while being both engrossed in your storytelling and marvelling at your magnificence. Make it easy for your audience, not difficult. Make them swoon. (Note: even if your articulation is good, you should at least warm up your organs before. This is so you don't trip up over your words or get a dry mouth.)

7. <u>Video capture it</u>. If you have a smart phone you have a video recorder. Record yourself practicing. Then watch the tape. As uncomfortable as that can be, watch the tape. After the initial squirm factor, consider what you would have thought about your speech as an audience member. Try to step outside your own needs and wants to achieve this. Then correct and re-record. Do it again. Repetition. Next gain feedback from outside. Get some candid feedback to help you.

8. <u>Keynote / PowerPoint show</u>. This tactic is also great for memorising your speech. First you put together a group of Keynote / PowerPoint slides made with large images. Then record an audio overlaying the file with what you want to say. Save it as a movie file. Play the movie repeatedly to both finalise the content, lock it in and then ultimately to embed the content in your mind. Whether you use the slides on the day is irrelevant. You could just use this as a learning and memorisation tool. Cool, hey?

9. <u>Repetition over time</u>. By working on these skills regularly, ideally daily, you can really refine and excel in them. There are networking and other groups where you can use the opportunity to speak to a new audience constantly. Speaking doesn't have to be just when there is a presentation coming up.

10. <u>Have help at hand</u>. Seek help from those who can ensure the presentation goes exceptionally well. Make sure all of the details are covered beforehand. Seek the details before the event. Work as a team member with the event planner. If your team is running the event, praise them, encourage them. These jobs can be stressful and thankless tasks.

Consider your habits. Think through what you could be better at doing. Write it down. Make that commitment to yourself to take steps to be more organised around your speaking.

Do you dedicate time to crafting your words and stories?

Professionals at the top of their game put in several hours every day to work on this. It is just like any athlete. You need to work at your craft regularly.

I enjoy Mark Twain's quote: 'It takes me three weeks to write an impromptu speech'.

I love this because it's so true. If you take something, let's say a rock from the ground. When you first find it, it can have rough edges, scratches and be a bit hazy. Then you take it home, give it a wash, polish it up, and voila. You have a shiny new pet rock.

The same goes for your speaking. Your words can be moulded. Take the example of a story. When you first write out a story, it can be so lengthy. It takes so long to cut through the noise of the story. In other words, what is important and what is not. To really sharpen the key parts of the story, you can easily go through and cut out words that don't have a place in the story.

Often there are wordy descriptions in there that do not serve the message. Stating the message in less than ten words is key. As Craig Valentine calls it, the Foundational Phrase. Cutting to the core is key.

I urge you to write out (or type out) your speech or your stories and put them apart. Have someone else review them. Have your coach work on them with you. What you don't want is too much blah blah blah. Too much narration. Too much information.

One of the mistakes I have made over the years has been to keep creating new stories while not continuing to craft the good ones too. As Darren LaCroix would say, start a story file. Have it on your desktop. Add to it regularly. Especially the humorous stories - write them down - every time they occur.

When it comes to speaking, there is more to it than the words coming out of your mouth, the gestures you use and the way that you command the stage. There is the preparation. The seconds, minutes, hours, days, weeks, months and years of crafting your words and your work to be on that stage with your masterpiece.

Thinking ahead is key. Consider where you will be speaking, with whom, for what purpose. Consider the 10 techniques for preparing for your presentation.

Write out a plan preparing for your speech. For example if your speech is ten weeks away, you could prepare a table format which contains what you will do each week in the lead up to the speech. This should include practice in front of people and getting feedback if possible.

Chapter Review:

In this chapter we have examined the following topics and learnings:

I.   <u>Explored how to bring the 'A' game to each presentation</u>. Especially that there are techniques that can help you to be your absolute best on the day (or night). We saw the example where Wendy had asked you to present to the Board, an important presentation, and yet there wasn't time to prepare - well there was but time wasn't allocated. We learnt the importance of WINGS not WING. Have your wings to fly as a speaker, don't leave it to the last minute and wing your presentation.

II. <u>Enjoyed the techniques for planning for speaking</u>. These are: (1) Book in time to prepare, (2) Tips for major keynote, (3) Plan your impromptu - yes it can be done, (4) Drill-drill-drill, (5) Plan your interactions - don't leave it to chance, (6) Improve elocution, (7) Video capture it - a most powerful activity to spark you into improvement, (8) Keynote show - awesome tool for practice, (9) Repetition over time, and (10) Have help at hand - you don't have to fly solo all the time.

III. <u>Examined the importance of dedicating time</u>. We looked into ways that you can dedicate your precious time to your speeches and stories. They don't magically appear as the world's greatest masterpieces, but can become that way through work, drilling, feedback and effort. Nurture those babies you create.

What about you?

_____

_____

_____

_____

_____

_____

Chapter 11

Excellent Timing

'Treat 3 people like 3000 and 3000 like 3.'

Kirk Fox

Chapter 11: Excellent Timing

Help. I've been allocated 30 minutes to deliver my presentation. How on earth am I expected to fit in all of my valuable content into such a short period of time?

Relax. You are not expected to. You only need to include what is relevant to this audience.

To be an effective speaker, you need to understand the value of time. Beyond this, you should strive to maximise the use of your moments on and off stage. You should strive for Excellent Timing.

Time is critical. We all have the same number of seconds, minutes, hours, weeks and months in the year. When you stop and seriously think about it, how are you using your:

- 168 hours in the week?

- 1440 minutes in a day?

- 31,536,000 seconds in a year?

Just as in life, and watching how and where you spend your time, so should you consider timing around your speaking. Here's a few ideas about how being smart with your time as a speaker can really add value to your life:

Table 16 – 5 Smart ways to maximise your time as a speaker

#	Smart Way	Detail	Tips
1	**Create 'Signature Speech'**	Create it once, craft and re-craft. Continue to refine your masterpiece (rather than creating new speeches each time).	Create your speech with the ability to articulate your core message. Seek feedback on your speech. Put the craft of speaking into it. Whether that is building in an impersonation or a poem or some element of surprise. Go beyond what is expected. Nurture it until it really is a masterpiece and is your signature speech.
2	**Plan ahead**	Organise your time OUTSIDE of your speech.	Know how long EVERYTHING else takes, such as: - driving to the venue. - setting up your equipment. - drinking water and bathroom stops. - being ready ahead of when your audience members arrive.

3	**Speech timing**	Organise your time INSIDE your speech.	- Be very clear how much time you have allocated for your intro, your blocks and your summary in closing.
		Break it down - organise your speech into five minute chunks and then you can construct it how you need to depending on how long you are being asked to present on.	- Break it down into five minute blocks.
			- Know how long each part takes to deliver while building in flexibility for when participants take longer than planned. Know where you can cut other parts short.
4	**Preparation**	Knowing who you are speaking to, doing your audience analysis (see chapter 1) and having the macro and micro view of the event.	- Know what the venue is.
			- Find out who the other speakers are.
			- Contact the other speakers to discuss what they are talking about and how you can work as a team.
			- Conduct your audience analysis (Chapter 5-Easy Structuring).

5	Stories	Hone your stories so that you know them so well, they fit like a glove.	- Have your core stories practiced so you know how long they take to deliver. - Make them succinct - choose and use your words carefully.

'Anna, but what about if I get there and.... everything gets changed?'

Adapting to changes in time

Here are my tips for when there are changes in the timing. The key is to roll with the changes, adapt and act like a professional at all times. Some things are just beyond your control and not all people are as organised as you certainly will be. Glitches do happen on the day.

1. <u>Remain cool and calm (Attitude)</u>. You getting upset about changes, such as your time being shortened, is not going to serve you well. You need to adapt in attitude and take it on the chin. Ok, it's not your fault and you are the victim of the change, just roll with it.

2. <u>Clarify</u>. Ok, so you've been told that you only have 30 minutes instead of 45. I suggest that you come up with your recommended use of the 30 minutes and then check in with the event organiser. This shows that you are first a good sport about it, and you are

being responsible about the value you are still able to give. It also shows that you are working in as a team player. No one can turn around later and say 'you said you would deliver 'x' and you didn't' etc.

3. <u>Let the audience in on it</u>. This must be done in a tactful way. Do not stand in front of your audience and say 'Well I only have 30 minutes now and not 45 minutes so I don't get to give you the value I had hoped...' etc. Do it more along the lines of: 'Ok, due to the changes today we now have 30 minutes to fit in the 45 minutes worth of value. Are you ready?' Treat it as an opportunity to increase the pace and get acceleration, rather than an excuse to just slacken off, slow down or worst of all BLAME others and switch off. No - accept the challenge with graciousness and rise to the occasion. Thrive on it.

4. <u>Follow-up</u>. Fine, you didn't get to deliver all your value. There must be a future opportunity for you to do so. Make sure you follow-up and let them know that you would be willing to come back and do another session to ensure the full value is achieved.

5. <u>Special offer</u>. A suggested add-on to tip 4 could be to give a special offer, e.g. discount on a product. For example, you could run a free webinar for them to cover off on the key learnings they didn't get exposed to on that day.

Techniques to help you manage time

Time can be a wonderful thing and also a limitation. What about when it is within your control to keep to time and things start getting out of hand?

This is where you shouldn't feel alone in having to do it all yourself. There are tools to help you track your time when speaking. I'm not saying you can be lazy here. I'm not saying that you should stand out front and waffle waffle waffle until you see your time is up. Gosh no.

What I mean is that you may be running one of your interactive sessions and you find that your audience is really getting into it. They love it. They are enjoying it so much and getting value out of the learning so much that you believe it is in this audience's interest to continue on a little longer than planned.

Never assume that your audience is ok with the idea of going over time. Always respect their time and consult them. One of the Branches I worked for in Government held a planning day at the end of each month. It was held off-site and was an opportunity for the team to have a strategic update and to receive education. On one occasion, a senior leader was on the program to come and visit to deliver an update about some of the changes happening in the organisation. The leader was late. He was late to the extent that he arrived right before the planned end time. Instead of identifying this point and addressing it, the leader simply ignored it and proceeded with his speech. The speech was a one sided information monologue with no new information. Not only were the audience disrespected for the time they lost, but the content did not hold true value. Ba-Bow.

One technique you can use here if you are faced with this situation is to seek your audience's permission to do so. You could stop them from what they are doing (for 30 seconds) and ask: 'Ok, we have a half hour to go and you seem to really be enjoying this session and getting a whole lot out of it. Hands up if you would like to continue on with this veritas session for an extra 10 minutes noting that there will be less time to spend on the voice activities?' Then get them to give you the feedback on it. The choice is with them. If they choose to keep going, no one can turn around later and accuse you of rushing through the voice session because you put the choice out to them. Instant feedback.

How to be succinct

Every word counts. When it comes to speaking, aim to be succinct. The reason for this is that when you are efficient with your words, you are received as more skilful and you are easier to understand. Being clear and deliberate with your words can mean the difference between going over and keeping within your allocated time. Here are some ways you can ensure that you are succinct:

- Plan your words.

- Drill your presentation.

- Remove the noise and filler words.

- Pause to give your audience time for key points to sink in.

- Craft your speech like a wordsmith. Write it out and seek ways of reducing words and for better expression.

Be aware that time can get away before our very eyes.

Chapter Review:

In this chapter we have examined the following topics and learnings:

I. <u>Explored time and the importance of making it count</u>. Each of us has the same number of seconds, hours, minutes and days in our week. Yet some seem to use it more effectively. How do you spend yours? How you plan your speech into the time allocated is so important for your credibility. Stick to time. ALWAYS.

II. <u>Seen 5 Smart ways to maximise your time as a speaker</u>. These smart ways are (1) Create your Signature Speech, (2) Plan ahead - every little detail, (3) Speech timing - make sure you know it inside and out, (4) Preparation - is always king, and (5) Stories - know how much time you need for a story and manage your speeches into blocks of 5 minutes to be added as needed.

III. <u>Adapted to changes in speech times - 5 tips</u>. In times where there are changes outside of your control, rather than being flustered and recriminating, you need to take it on the chin and adapt. Quickly. Like the professional that you are. The five tips: (1) Attitude - keep it in check at all times, (2) Clarify - what is ok to rush through so they still get full value -

obtain client / audience input, (3) Let audience in - no blaming, just cooperation, (4) Follow-up - so they can have more of you later, and (5) Special offer - give give give.

IV.   Recognised that Time is Gold. Cherish it.

V.   <u>Reviewed how to be succinct</u>.   Through solid preparation and planning for a presentation, you can ensure that your words are deliberate, efficient and easier to receive and understand by your audience.

What about you?

Chapter 12

Elevate

'If you have an important point to make, don't try to be subtle or clever.
Use a pile driver. Hit the point once. Then come back and hit it again.
Then hit it a third time – a tremendous whack.'

Winston S. Churchill

Chapter 12: Elevate

People want to belong to, or experience something that elevates them. A human can do so much, yet when held up by others, when supported by more than just yourself, wonderful things can be achieved.

There are so many examples of this. Let's take one: Australian singer and actress Kylie Minogue. We see Kylie up on stage in her sparkling costumes, perfectly placed hair and makeup, and choreographed moves. It is a sight to hear and see.

What we do hear and see is of course the finished product. The end result of countless hours on stage. Practicing and perfecting the moves to all the routines.

Kylie does not achieve this level of performance on her own. Kylie has a support team that helps her, to build her up and to ensure that when she is on stage, everything is in place. From choreographers to makeup to sound. Each sequin glitters as it should and each move is delivered with ease (or at least it looks like it is). Of course Kylie is a true professional with years of practice in perfecting her craft as well.

Whether it is a seasoned performer like Kylie Minogue, or you and I, we all need a team around us that will take us to that next level.

When you are speaking, you can give the gift to your audience of lifting them to that next level. To elevate them. To a place where they didn't realise they could go.

I have been hearing the message a lot that you need to build a community for people to belong to. To connect with and get them engaged. When this happens they feel good and they feel elevated because they are a part of something bigger than themselves.

I can't help but think that this is something that was made up by extroverts. I agree that people do need to feel a sense of community and belonging, though I don't believe that learning has to be a community activity. I think on the flip side we also have the need to learn things fast. And without interference. We just need to know how to do it. And we don't necessarily want to have to sit in a classroom for days on end to do so.

Here are some questions for you to consider:

How do you feel about learning for you?

Do you prefer to learn with others?

How do you elevate an audience?

As a speaker, you can find a way to elevate your audience. This can be done a number of ways. Here are a few:

Table 17 - Top 11 ways to elevate others

1	**Build a community**	Build a community so that they can engage with each other, share the learnings and feel like they are a part of something bigger. Make it positive, fun, supportive and uplifting.
2	**Treat them well**	This sounds silly, but many people have not been treated well in the past and to treat them well is refreshing. What this means is to recognise them for their achievements, celebrate them and help them find what is great about them, what is unique and how to bring that out. For example, if you can help someone discover how they can make money from something they love to do so that they don't have to work in a dead-end job, they are going to be pretty happy about that.
3	**Key learnings**	Educational material that teaches them new skills or ways of thinking. Knowledge that they can keep in a way that is simple enough to understand and also memorable, hits the mark.
4	**A system**	A system containing 'how to' steps which can help with the practical application of the learning and that is easy to remember.
5	**New information**	Your fresh take on a subject.
6	**Free content**	Articles, white paper.

7	Free e-book	If you have a published book, create an e-book, a condensed version of the book and give it away. Your audience will find great value in this and it can help them to sample your teachings and what you believe in. Your take on your subject.
8	Free gift	Give them a gift in your keynote or training session. Such as blowing bubbles, a pen or novelty item. This could be your signature prop. It goes a long way to them remembering you. It should tie in to your teachings.
9	Free assessment	On their skills.
10	Free lists	E.g. top ten engagement tips.
11	Message with meaning	Foundational phrase that changes their life.

Another key way to elevate your audience is to build a community. If there is a common goal within your audience, or multiple audiences, you can build a community where they can connect, and continue to learn and grow. For example, I have a Speakers' Club, where my community can sign up and be a part of a community that learns together and shares among each other.

This in turn, elevates them to a new level where they can be out there sharing their message with their audiences.

People want to be a part of a community that elevates them.

You can provide them the foundation to do this.

Professional Speaking

You want to be in this game as a full time occupation. Here are tips that I have learnt along the way.

Table 18 – Speaker types – how to profit professionally from speaking

1	**Keynote speaker**	Deliver a keynote speech at a convention. Speak for a fee. Speak to larger audiences. Be the opening or closing speaker at the conference, rather than someone running a breakout session. This is a person who is an influencer, who has a strong message and a core identity that shines through.
2	**Trainer**	Some who educates and trains in the classroom setup. A person who runs seminars, courses and trains on skills.
3	**Facilitator**	A professional who guides through the process of the meeting. Keeping it on track, on point and to time. Ensuring that the outcomes are met.
4	**Webinar and online trainer**	A trainer who delivers specifically via the medium of a webinar or via online training.
5	**Coach**	A coach who speaks, educates and imparts knowledge in a number of ways. One who motivates, guides and enables not only their 'stars', but every participant, regardless of ability.

6	**Online and Membership site educator**	A professional who runs a membership site which involves videos and online learning. Example: The Speakers Club.
7	**Talk show host**	In this category, you could be a talk show host who is hosting an online program such as on YouTube.

There are many ideas now given we have the online dynamic, here are just a few to consider. There doesn't seem to be a 'one size fits all' solution. It comes down to what works for you.

Chapter Review:

In this chapter we have examined the following topics and learnings:

I. <u>Explored the idea that people want to be elevated</u>. People want to feel a part of something bigger than them. You can create this for them. This can be done in many different ways. We looked at the example of Kylie Minogue who is a superstar on stage yet she does not do this alone. It takes many people to create something special. What will you create for your people?

II. <u>Examined the 11 ways to elevate others</u>. These are (1) Build a community - that people can feel a part of, (2) Treat them well - people want positive influence in their life, (3) Key learnings - give them something to take away and apply straight away, (4) A System - people want something simple to follow that makes their life easier and removes pain, (5) New information - or a fresh take on an old topic, (6) Free content - give away your thoughts to see if these gel with their own, so they can get to know your take on your topic, (7) Free e-book, (8) Free gift, (9) Free assessment - to help them to decide on the help they need, (10) Free lists - to help them, and (11) Message with meaning - something to take away today and be a better person tomorrow.

III.   <u>Viewed 7 different types of professional speakers</u>. We have (1) Keynote presenter, (2) Trainer, (3) Facilitator, (4) Webinar / online trainer, (5) Coach, (6) Membership educator, and (7) Talk show host. These are just some of the roles going today and there are more being created regularly as new technologies become available.

What about you?

_____

_____

_____

_____

_____

_____

_____

Summary

This book has been a journey through speaking. Through its nuances, details and crafting areas. Who would have thought that standing up in front of a group of people, opening your mouth and having words come out could have so much skill to it? And yet, it really isn't that difficult. When you know the how.

Yes. It really is time that help is out there for EVERY person who knows in their heart of hearts, that a presentation looms. A presentation that may come around today, tomorrow or next year. Either way, whenever it comes, why not be on top of it, in front of it, facing it head on saying 'come right over'. Rather than running the other way screaming.

It's also time to lift up those who already speak, yet help hasn't been easily and readily at hand. Now it is.

We can make public speaking FUN (truly). If they were doing and talking about rhetoric and speaking and the art of persuasion over 2,000 years ago, we can be conquering it today. We can be taking it by the horns, or in this case the words, and getting them out there. The right words at the right time for our audience, because we considered what they needed, worked it through using our expertise, and then handed it to them on a platter.

Yes, customer service does go hand in hand with being a speaker. It is a privilege. It is about serving the audience. It is about having grace, eloquence and style. And it is about having a core message that can move them to a better place in their world. The blend of style and substance. That is a true orator.

Can you just imagine what you can do to influence change in your world when you are a confident, practiced, polished orator? Even just a little bit further practiced than where you are today could boost your results in what you want to achieve in life.

Before we part (for now), I offer you the gift of the alphabet of public speaking. These 1-3 words for each letter in the alphabet are designed to remind you what is important to keep in mind in all you do in your speaking. These little snippets will help prompt you to do certain things. For example: 'Negate nerves' = to not let them get to you, keep them at bay, rise above them and conquer. 'Invite Interaction' = have your audience engage with you, don't just talk at them, invite them into the content that is all for them. 'Wings not Wing' = don't wing your presentation, get your speaking wings and take flight proudly so you can soar the skies.

Speakers: Spread your wings and soar the skies. I'll be with you all the way.

In Summary, here are the three Vs again:

Table 19 – Summary of the 3 Vs to Victory Via Voice

#	3 Vs	Description	Questions to ask yourself
1	**VALUE**	Make sure your presentations are All About Audience.	*What is the Value you can bring your audience?* *What are your 3 qualities that represent your speaking style?*
2	**VERITAS**	Bring out the 'real you'. - Your truth - is who you really are coming out? - Honing the 'YOU'. - Stories. - Authenticity - bringing out the human being you are. - Honesty - if you have to ask them to do something difficult.	*How is my audience getting to know me?* *Are the stories I use helping to bring out veritas for me?*

3	VOICE	Bring out the power in Voice, the Carrier of Your unique sound.	*Is your voice congruent with your message and / or your leadership style?*
		In particular: - Tones. - Maximising your message. - Emphasis - on words and sounds. - Variety of sound. - Pitch. - Pace. - Volume.	*How do you use elements of voice to enhance your message?*

Public Speaking Alphabet

Here's a little gift I made just for you (*oooh excitement*). To take with you, these sayings are very much key to keeping you on track with your speaking. If you follow them in spirit, you will maintain the right path. Here t'is.

Table 20 - Public Speaking Alphabet

A	=	**All About Audience**	Always deliver value to your audience.
B	=	**Ban Boring**	Don't do public speaking the old way.
C	=	**Create Change**	As a speaker, you are an Agent of Change.
D	=	**Deliver Diversely**	Think of different ways to deliver your content.
E	=	**Energise**	Bring incredible energy to your audience.
F	=	**Forge Through Fear**	Lose fear. It only exists because we mistakenly think it does.

G	=	**Gift to Gain**	To Gift is to Lift. When you gift your audience you gain.
H	=	**Have Humour**	Create humorous moments in your presentation.
I	=	**Invite Interaction**	Do it early and often.
J	=	**Joyful Joyful**	Enjoy thine speaking.
K	=	**Keep knowing**	Keep your knowledge up and be learning always.
L	=	**Lift Levels**	Help lift your audience to rise to a new level.
M	=	**Manoeuvre with a Mission**	When moving on stage, Manoeuvre with a Mission.
N	=	**Negate Nerves**	Let's remove those darned little suckers forever. Channel positivity.
O	=	**Organised Oratory**	Value the skill of oratory.
P	=	**Preparation**	Prepare Prepare Prepare.

Q	=	**Quest Quietly**	Be humble, don't grandstand yourself, keep 'I'-itus away.
R	=	**Respect**	Respect your audience and yourself.
S	=	**Storytime**	Put effort into bringing your stories to life.
T	=	**Teach Techniques**	Teach them a system and how to apply it.
U	=	**Unlimited**	Never put a ceiling on your speaking.
V	=	**Victor Via Voice**	Have the courage to speak.
W	=	**Wings, not Wing**	Don't just wing it, grow your speaking wings.
X	=	**Xtra Xtra!**	Always give your audience more.
Y	=	**Yes to You**	Use You a lot when conversing with your audience.
Z	=	**Zesty Zoom**	Never run out of zesty zoom for your audience.

Anna's Vocal Warm Ups

1. Can a happy dad have a bad day? Capable like a straight whale tail.

2. We eat cream cheese. Even in the eastern sea.

3. Kittens with mittens are forbidden to fish in Italy.

4. Alan is able to appreciate angels aged above eighty eight.

5. Try to bite a bit of big blue bunyip. Brandish beautiful bananas and berries.

6. Horrible hikers have hot heads half her height.

7. Gee, Graham has a great grey grain and grizzly goose game.

8. Quirky quacks require the queen to retreat rather quickly.

9. Look for food in the noodle pond in Scotland and beyond.

10. Harry and Henry, Larry and Jerry, Shelley Sally Sue Santangelo.

11. Cruise for clues, don't lose your blue and purple shoes.

12. Robots require really robust revenue raising to wrestle and rescue rabbits.

13. It is a tiny biscuit with thin mint filling.

14. We wash weekly with wiry weasels, while waiting, wearing white and whistling.

15. Yellow is mellow like a soft marshmallow fellow.

16. Think thoughtfully thorough thoughts while thanking Ethel.

17. Mice like to find time to sit on wire and drink rice wine.

18. You, your youth yelps and yawps 'yes you yucky yelper'.

19. A sweet sauce is succulent; sometimes swilling in summer, settling softly and sizzling.

20. Why was Warren waiting with worry, while Wally wandered without wondering?

21. Vivid livid vicarious vices and vixens veered vivaciously.

22. Funny fella fights foreign furballs furiously and frantically.

23. Sorry is such a sweet and sour sensation, seeming soft and silent.

24. Zebras can play extra jazz sessions on the zingy xylophone with pizazz.

25. Nuts under stuff is enough to bluff and end up in the rough cup of love.

26. Cupid was aiming his arrow and holding heart for yield among merry men.

27. Bubbles smother the mother's chocolate crackles with sprinkles and crinkles.

28. The bright bluebird chirped happily while the brown grizzly bear bellowed.

29. Spiders sit scouring their surroundings before scaring species with simply their sight.

30. A camel tried to fly a kite but got spied on by the broody goose.

31. Why did the dainty duck deliver the dew to your yellow wheelbarrow?

32. The humble bumble bee meets the brown grizzly bear.

Acknowledgements

I've travelled far and wide to meet special people around the world. My gratitude goes to:

Philip Bendeich, for supporting me 100% every day.

Margaret and Ray, for being loving and supportive parents.

Colleen Sturgill and Frank, in sunny California, for a perfect paradise to write.

Darren LaCroix, for life changing inspiration at the 2010 Humor Bootcamp.

Mark Hunter, for being a true craftsman of the thoughtful spoken word.

Eric Pace, for expanding what's possible in High Performance Thinking - keep it alive.

Rodney Marks, for being hilarious and a shining light in the service of others.

Martin Brooker for setting a high example of courage in leadership.

Professional Speakers Australia, for providing a home for those who dare to dream and live the platform life: Phil Preston, Karen Armstrong, Jenny Cartwright, Gill Walker, Nina Sunday, Julie Garland-McLellan, Catherine Palin-Brinkworth, Lisa McInnes-

Smith. To the speakers on the Main Stage who make you laugh, cry, live and learn.

My PSA masterminders Adrian Spear, Georgina Adams and Sam Ades. SAGA!

Petter L Miller, for recognising the best in me and for your mentorship. I'm humbled.

Doug Campbell, for being an editor extraordinaire.

Karen and Richard Stacey for being timeless, consistent and classic leaders.

Heartfelt thank you to Toastmasters International and the many members for support and encouragement. Special mention to Jan Vecchio, Joan Rinaldi, David Fisher, Wendy White, Kaylene Ledgar, Ward Penman, Rick Haynes, Mike and Lesley Storkey and Mohammed Murad.

Paddy Kennedy for being a crusader in communication excellence.

Jana Barnhill for being such an inspirational communicator - world leaders should take note - you set a glowing example to the world.

Ally Mosher, for your rock solid patience and attentiveness. You're a gem.

Anna Perdriau MBA works wonders with your presentation and your speaking style. Anna's specialty is to bring out the magic in your public speaking so that you can connect with, and create change in your audience. As a result you save time, money and reduce stress with your speaking.

Anna is obsessed with helping people to connect with and create change in their audience through public speaking. Anna has delivered hundreds of speeches to live audiences. As a keen student of speaking, she has attended the world championship of public speaking five years in a row in the USA and Malaysia. Anna has travelled across the USA to see and be trained by some of the world's best speakers in the National Speakers Association.

Anna has earned a Master of Business Administration from the University of South Australia International School of Business and a Bachelor of Communications from Griffith University. Anna held significant responsibility as a Project Director in the Australian Government where at the height of her career, she was the youngest civilian female to manage a billion dollar acquisition program. Anna is the membership manager for Professional Speakers Australia NSW.

What's my next step?

For more information, please visit

www.speakingexcellence.co

Leave your name and email for exciting updates
and free stuff!

or contact me at

anna@destinationexcellence.com.au

Coaching: the fastest way to excellence

www.ingramcontent.com/pod-product-compliance
Lightning Source LLC
Chambersburg PA
CBHW071250220526
45468CB00001B/69